Enjoying The
Courtship & Marital Dances
Now and Evermore

John F. Paugstat

WestBow Press books may be ordered through booksellers or by contacting:

WestBow Press
A Division of Thomas Nelson & Zondervan
1663 Liberty Drive
Bloomington, IN 47403
www.westbowpress.com
844-714-3454

ISBN: 978-1-6642-8565-1 (sc)
ISBN: 978-1-6642-8567-5 (hc)
ISBN: 978-1-6642-8566-8 (e)

Library of Congress Control Number: 2022922193

Print information available on the last page.

WestBow Press rev. date: 02/20/2023

WestBow
PRESS®
A DIVISION OF THOMAS NELSON
& ZONDERVAN

Author's Note

The Bible verses in this text serve as a useful reference and ready guide for daily behavior in a marital relationship. The references are rooted in the King James Version (KJV). However, to make the verses compatible with current English voice, all scripture is quoted, paraphrased, or summarized from some twenty Bible versions.

For example, all thees and thous of the KJV have been changed to modern English forms. Extraneous words and phrases are eliminated or reduced to the simplest form. (See detail in the appendix covering the Biblical Behavioral Instructions.)

Each verse is identified with the closest version from which it is quoted or paraphrased. The default version has its roots in the Modern King James Version (MKJV).

Acknowledgments

Carol Musser
For her insightful comments and suggestions on the text.

Darlene Paugstat (wife of the author)
For her patience and encouragement in the writing of this book.

The Editors and Support Team of WestBow Press
For their suggestions toward a more reader-friendly text.

I had a good marriage
That could have been better,
Had the author (my husband),
Written this book before our marriage.
Darlene Paugstat

Marital "Blooms"

A Fit Marital Dancer
**Intuitively Performs
To the Music of Agape Love and
To the Biblical Choreography.**

Dance Magnificently
And Always with Joy.

Take-Home Challenge
**Be the Fit Mate
With the Integrity and Character
That You Desire in Your Mate.**

Why?
**A Joyful Marital Dance
Is Life at Its Finest.**

"I could have danced all night...
And still have begged for more.
I could have spread my wings
And done a thousand things
I never done before."

From My *Fair Lady* by A.J. Lerner, 1956

The Two
Shall Dance as One
Paraphrased—Mat 19:5

The author and his wife on their sixtieth wedding anniversary
Cover Page: Their wedding day

**Purpose: To review the fundamentals that ensure
An enduring, delightful Marital Dance.**

Table of Contents

The First Dance

I wrote the following letter to my mother (we called her Momma in German) after my first dance with my wife-to-be. The letter was lost in the files of antiquity until my children found and shared it on our fiftieth wedding anniversary. The letter portrays the wonders when boy discovers girl. In the letter, Bill is my brother. Introductory statements are left out.

After sixty-plus years, that dance is still going strong.

April 7, 1956

Dear Momma,

… I suppose that you heard about Bill. It is too bad, for he seemed so sensible, and now he wants to spend the rest of his life with one woman. That's a long time, Momma. I think that you are right; Bill should have listened to you. Like I told Bill, I am going to listen to you, Mom, and I am going to be strong and leave the women alone.

One thing though, I went to Reedley [CA] over the weekend and stayed at the home of a friendly Christian family. It just happened that they have a daughter about my age who took it upon herself to entertain me. Her father let me use his car, filled it with gas, and let me take it up into the mountains. Their daughter got into the car with me. I couldn't tell her to stay home since I was their guest. So I took her along, and away we went. I enjoyed driving that car, and the scenery was great—inside and outside of the car.

On Easter Sunday morning, their little daughter knocked on my door at about five o'clock in the morning. I got up, and before long, there she was beside me in the car on the way to Easter Sunrise Service. It was a beautiful morning, a little cold and cloudy but beautiful. The service was held high up where you could see over the whole valley. Then we had church breakfast, church service, and then to her home for a delightful Easter dinner.

When I went back to school at Berkeley [CA], they sent a nice piece of Angel Food Cake plus lots of cookies, but they kept their little daughter. (I thought that they would have shared one of their two daughters.) That was all right, wasn't it, Momma? If they want to give me all that stuff and be nice to me—then why not enjoy? So I said, "John, it's Easter, and this kind mother has two daughters and no sons. So make her feel good and act like her son. So I did, but it was a sacrifice on my part. You know how it is. That's OK, isn't it Momma—to be nice to old ladies with lovely daughters? See, I am not like Bill. It's just that some old ladies happen—well, you know.

Don't worry about me, Momma. I figure that as long as I am nice to the old ladies, I'm OK. It is 2:15 AM Sunday.

Good night,

Your youngest son—John

1

Preface

Long ago, a wise man declared that there are four things too wonderful for me:

    The way of an eagle in the air;

    The way of a snake on a rock;

    The way of a ship in the middle of the sea;

    And the way of a man with a maiden.   (Pro 30:18, 19)

Those ways are worthy of wonder. However, there is a fifth way, more wondrous than all.

    Man and maiden make two, and the two become one.

    United as one, they have one after one,

    becoming one family under one God.

That wonder and power of marital unity are foundational to this book. It is difficult to imagine any discussion of greater interest, mystery, beauty, and majesty. Indeed, the pinnacle of all wonders is embedded in that mysterious union of man and woman in a lifetime Marital Dance resulting in one family under one God. That is the ideal—the objective.

The word *dancing*, as used in this book, symbolizes the way of life. The *Marital Dance* relates to the way of life after the wedding ceremony.

The above has an interesting anomaly and caveat. As the following anecdote shows, creating a marital masterpiece is easier than preserving it.

A friend and I were riding our cycles through Kentucky's beautiful bluegrass countryside. We stopped to admire a picturesque, pastoral setting that featured an old arched bridge crossing a gentle, serene creek defined by wildflowers and cattle lazily grazing nearby. He asked me to leave so that he could have some romantic time alone with *His Love*. The seed was sown; the romance blossomed. Several months later, I was privileged to attend their lovely wedding ceremony, which was capped by mutual promises "to love and cherish until death do us part." They seemed compatible, with shared values and interests; they had pleasing personalities and enjoyed a solid Christian heritage. As the saying goes, "It was a marriage made in heaven."

For the rest of the story, move the clock forward about ten years. At a social gathering, my cycle friend angrily confronted me for having invited *her*—his ex-love, ex-wife, and his child's mother. I was unprepared for that dramatic, surreal shift in such a short period. How could a marriage made in heaven be dissolved in such a short time with such hostile feelings? What went wrong and why? This book addresses those questions, including means to ensure a joyful, enduring Marital Dance.

The divorce rate in the Christian community is on par with the secular community, which has varied between 14 percent and 25 percent over the last decade. That reality represents a dramatic paradigm shift in foundational Christian marital values and behavior. That reality indicates that the Christian way has no merit over the secular in producing a happy and lasting marital relationship. If that is true, why this book?

In response, faulty results are due to a faulty standard, understanding, or application. From the scientific and the biblical perspectives, if we properly apply time-proven basics, we can count on and enjoy the consequential benefits. That reality is foundational to this book. Indeed, all man's fantastic developments are based on the application of time-proven principles. Failure to understand or properly apply those principles can result in catastrophic events.

The book *UnChristian* by David Kinnaman notes that most Christians do not know the basics of their faith and therefore cannot apply or benefit from them. The stats indicate that a verbal Christian without practice has no advantage in a marital relationship over a non-Christian. That cause/effect reality says it all.

To enjoy a lifetime Marital Dance, we need to know and correctly apply time-proven basics to ensure the desired results. Failure to understand or correctly apply truth can result in catastrophic events leading to destruction and death. Accordingly, this book champions the time-proven Biblical Behavioral Instructions (BBI) that detail the music, choreography, and behavioral guidelines basic to an enduring, enjoyable Marital Dance.

The need for an in-depth response to marital issues became a personal challenge. Seemingly overnight, my grandchildren morphed into young adults with critical lifetime decisions to make. One of the most critical decisions has to do with the selection of a mate. As my heritage to them and now the reader, this book details what I learned from my marriage, vocation, studies, and observation, and from the Bible.

In a positive and beneficial marital relationship, the two shall become as one, and that one shall multiply and become many, as in one family. A family consists of a father, mother, children, and relatives, in which each has a unique personality and needs. The challenge is to have the diverse parts work together in harmonious unity. To meet that challenge, enter my expertise in systems development, which provides the basics toward developing a functional family, in which the members mesh and are mutually supportive of a common good and goal.

The objectives of a family are to remain functional and improve with time. To ensure a functional family relationship, enter my expertise in Quality Enhancement. Quality includes a set of principles and procedures designed to ensure ongoing, ever-improving fitness for use. To ensure a high-quality marital union, I outlined the New Testament several times, pulling and consolidating all references relating to a marital relationship. The resulting BBI are presented in Appendix I.

My expertise in systems development, quality enhancement, and biblical application brings a unique perspective to the subject of marital fitness. The intent is to supply the husband and wife with time-proven principles and behavioral guidelines so that they can become proficient dancers in an enjoyable, lifetime Marital Dance to the limits of their bent, talents, and capabilities.

In a marital relationship, the concept of *dancing as one* is a picture presentation that most can appreciate and emulate. The picture details the time-tested BBI toward perfection. The related detail can be daunting, but look at it positively. That detail promises a Marital Dance at the ultimate level. As you practice and improve, you will enjoy a good dance today and a better dance tomorrow—regardless of the circumstances. The proof is in the pudding. My wife and I have enjoyed dancing as one for more than sixty years, thanks in part to the writing of this book and to the willful practice of time-proven precepts as championed in the BBI.

The Marital-Dance Fitness Test

An enjoyable Marital Dance requires that you and your spouse are compatible in core values and proficient in the dance music and choreography. To enjoy the Marital Dance to the max, periodically take the following Fitness Test to determine potential areas for improvement.

Each of the fourteen items in the test is critical to the enjoyment of the Marital Dance. Deficiency in any area will result in a subpar Marital Dance.

As you become proficient dancers, you may feel that there is little to no room for improvement. However, as the following photo suggests, even when you are seemingly picture-perfect, there is always room for improvement. Indeed, the better you become, the better you want to be, and the more opportunity you will see for improvement.

The objective is a second-nature response in each area—good today and better tomorrow. The following test is also a summary of the subject matter in this book.

(Almost) Picture-Perfect
How can I improve toward a better tomorrow?

The Ultimate Test
Master, search us,
and see if there is any fault in us.
(Paraphrased from Psa 139: 23–24)

The Fitness Test

Do We Know for Instinctive Use and Application:

1. ***The Basics of our Faith?***
   To ensure that we dance to the same choreography

2. ***The Music of Agape Love?***
   To ensure that we feel and intuitively dance to the same music

3. ***The Biblical Instructions for Marital Behavior?***
   To ensure unity in the Marital Dance

4. ***Our Goals and Objectives and How to Make Them Happen?***
   To ensure that we dance as one toward a common goal

5. ***The Disciplines of a Healthy Lifestyle?***
   To ensure a vibrant, inspirational, exemplary dance to physical limits

6. ***The Dynamics of Communication?***
   To enable mutual understanding and effect positive changes

7. ***The Dynamics of Conflict Resolution?***
   To bring peace and harmony to the Marital Dance

8. ***The Basics of Valid Decision-Making?***
   To avoid the stresses and tragedies of wrong decisions

9. ***The Basics of Discernment: When Right Fades into Wrong?***
   To ensure valid decisions in all areas of life

10. ***The Basics of the Christian Marital Dance?***
    To enjoy a good marriage and avoid the bitter cup and costs of divorce

11. ***The Basics of Time, Money, and Mind Management?***
    To enjoy the economic and social benefits of marriage and avoid the stress of insolvency

12. ***The Basics of Priority, Balance, and Finish?***
    To effectively apply our limited resources toward maximized benefits

13. ***Means to Effect a Positive Social Environment?***
    To experience the Marital Dance in a pleasant, conducive environment

14. ***Our Partners' Talents, Abilities, and Core Values?***
    To ensure a unified Marital Dance with maximized, synergistic gain

Chapter 1

The Way of Man with Maiden

The Way of Man with Maiden is a wonder of wonders that goes back to First-Man, who lived in a gorgeous garden called Eden. (This story is a paraphrased account of the first man and woman, Adam and Eve, as recorded in Genesis 1:26 to Gen 2:15.)

First-Man had all he wanted but was sad for reasons he knew not. His Maker saw the sadness and knew what was missing. He put First-Man into a deep sleep and then created a helpmate and companion for First-Man. When finished, He declared His final creation to be very good, the most exquisite of all His creations. First-Man should be pleased.

When First-Man awakened from his sleep, the Creator's masterpiece was at his side. That masterpiece was a young maiden—so like First-Man, yet so eloquently different. These two, the first man and woman, defined and enjoyed the first Courtship Dance.

In time, the Creator asked First-Man how he liked his new companion. "Oh, she is gorgeous! Her voice, her eyes, and her touch are the most lovely and magnificent of all Your creations. Thank you for giving me such a beautiful gift."

The Master Creator looked at His ultimate creations: the first man and woman. He was pleased by what He heard and saw; He blessed them and said unto them, "Multiply and fill the earth."

And so was born the first Marital Dance, the seedbed for all humanity.

The Trail of Wonders

As a wee laddie buck, I squeezed memory to its limits and came to a startling conclusion: since I could not remember a beginning, I had always existed. I was part of an immortal family comprised of my masters (called *Poppa* and *Momma* in German), my superiors (older brothers), and my younger sisters (who, unfortunately for me, were girls). When I was a small boy, life was all wonder. If I was immortal, what did it mean to have a birthday? Why was I only six years old? Why were my sisters physically different?

The answer to those fundamental wonders of life hit the pride of my being with hurricane force. Within a short period of maybe ten minutes, I was reduced from the majestic state of immortality to the status of a mere mortal—with a beginning more humble than the limits of my imagination.

I was picking strawberries with a new friend, as wee a lad as I. As boys often do, he expounded on his knowledge by explaining the facts of life in graphic detail. What he said was unbelievable to an immortal such as I. No way! Maybe what he related was true for him but not for me. If I had a beginning, it was surely nobler than what he described. In response to my unbelief, he assured me that all he said was true since his parents had demonstrated the details. From the perspective of a boy, my trail of wonders had a lowly beginning.

If my friend was right, then my father and mother defined my origin. That didn't go over well in the mind of this boy. To start me, my poppa and momma had to be *intimate.* No way! I never saw my father touch my mother in affection, let alone in an intimate embrace. I knew my mother; she would not tolerate any embrace from Poppa. They slept in separate bedrooms, making intimate embrace impossible. Moreover, there were six of us kids. It was unthinkable that Poppa and Momma had ever touched in a single voluntary, intimate embrace, let alone been intimate six times. Those realities settled it: my strawberry-picking friend suffered from nightmarish hallucinations that he took for real.

That was the beginning of my journey on the trail of wonders. The next wonder was the dramatic change in me that I could not have imagined as a boy. That mysterious wonder started early in life when I learned that there were two types of people: boys and girls. As a boy, I could not understand why God created girls and women. Girls were icky, without reason or benefit—at least that is how they looked through this boy's eyes.

In time, I experienced a strange and disturbing change. Occasionally, I gave a second look at some of the young maidens, and then a third look. What was going on? Unbelievably, I developed a strong desire to have one of those strange creatures for my own. My boyhood memories blushed in disbelief at that reality. The icky became desirable as gooey batter turned into chocolate cake.

With that reality, I was introduced to and became part of the delightful Courtship Dance that led to the mysterious Marital Dance, when I became one with an icky one and wondrously lived happily ever after. After sixty-plus years, we are still dancing as one.

How Mysterious and Marvelous Are Your Wonders, Oh Lord!

Marital Realities

The Courtship and Marital Dances have many faces, from the beautiful and graceful to the awkward and uncoordinated. In its worst form, the Marital Dance can be vulgar, degrading, and even deadly. Most marital jokes relate to the negative perception of marriage, as illustrated by the following jokes taken from memory.

- It is tragic: Jane and Harry never knew true happiness until they married. Then it was too late; their fate was sealed.
- The best way to learn your faults is to get married.
- Remember, when you have the last word with your spouse, that was your last word.

The above are humorous because they have an element of truth. Still, they raise a troubling question: How can the intensity of first love turn so quickly to dislike and even hate? The answer is complex, but it has its roots in reality.

Love is pure. Unattended, it easily turns rancid. Rancid love is relatively common, as confirmed by the high divorce rate. Unfortunately, rancid love can easily turn into deadly hate that often shows itself in suicide and murder. Tragically, I know of six people who died due to stale love that turned toxic and out of control. Fortunately, my father's faith, according to his words, saved my mother from being victim number seven in my circle of friends and relatives.

The above is similar to some medicinal ads that promise good health and then declare that the medicine can result in severe illness even unto death. With that reality, who needs the medicine? Likewise, who needs marriage that can result in emotional carnage and the termination of a sacred relationship?

In keeping with this book, Matthew 19:5–6 paraphrased says: The two shall [dance] as one. What God has joined together let no man disassemble.

From the above, marriage comes with the highest credentials:

Marriage was born in the mind of God.

The Biblical Marital Dance

The Marital Dance relates to the way of life after the wedding ceremony. After you say the traditional "I do," the Marital Dance begins. From that point forward, the Marital Dance is what you and your spouse make it.

Dancing is a dynamic performance to the beat of music and a prescribed set of procedures defined by choreography. Dancing has many faces, from the beautiful and graceful to the degrading and vulgar. Dancing is like a white sheet of paper—pure and clean but easily soiled. Keeping the Marital Dance white is the objective.

Basics of a beautiful and graceful dance:
- Music, which sets the rhythm and tempo
- Choreography, which defines the composition and arrangement of the dance
- Dancers who perform to the music and choreography

Basics of the biblical Marital Dance:
- The music is agape love, magnificently described in 1 Corinthians 13
- The behavior and choreography are defined in the Biblical Behavioral Instructions (BBI) of the New Testament
- The husband and wife are united and dance as one

The unity of husband and wife in the Marital Dance is summarized below

> The two shall leave their parents, hold fast to each other,
> And become one flesh, and be mutually submissive.
> (Eph 5:21–23, Mat 19:3–12)

The husband has the responsibility to lead the Marital Dance. He is to protect the interests and life of his mate—with his life if necessary. With her interests secured, the wife willingly submits to and follows her husband's lead. Their mutual submission to the will of God consummates their union to each other.

Note that the centerpiece of a marital relationship is Unity, which is expressively portrayed as *one flesh*. Unity has merit only when you and your spouse voluntarily accept and merge personal interests and desires to become one flesh.

So let us get on with it: the biblical way of man with maiden.

Unity

Unity is the number one biblical basic toward ensuring marital harmony. To be of one flesh, the couple must be unified in faithfulness, fitness, compatibility, and the like. If a couple is not unified as one flesh, their marital relationship is, at best, coexistence.

Our bodies serve as an excellent example of Unity. A healthy body is characterized by all the body parts functioning in harmony with the needs of the body. Similarly, a healthy relationship is characterized by the husband and wife functioning in harmony with the needs of the marital body. Toward a beautiful and harmonious Marital Dance, the husband and wife meld as one mind, one body, and one spirit, all under one God.

To appreciate the essence of Unity, consider the musical *Fiddler on the Roof.* The leading character, Tevye, asks his wife a question that goes to the heart and soul of Unity: "Do you love me?"

In reply, Tevye's wife notes that she prepares his meals, cleans his house, takes care of his children, and does many more chores to his benefit. By her reasoning, her actions show and prove her love.

Tevye acknowledges her devotion to duty but again asks, "Yes, but do you love me?" The cycle repeats several times, always ending with the same haunting question: "Yes, but do you love me?"

Tevye's wife proved her devotion to duty by attending to his needs. Tevye knew that. He did not know whether her love was from the heart or out of obligation. Did Tevye's wife think of herself as one with Tevye? Did Tevye occupy center place in her heart? Were they united, or did they coexist for mutual benefit? Did she accept Tevye, warts and all, as being one with her?

Unity is the consummation of agape love in action. Unity is the complete submission of self to another and accepting that other as being one with you. That leads to the ultimate objective: to be one in faith, core values, goals, objectives, joy, sorrow, pain, and suffering. As one, your freedoms are enhanced by the strengths of your spouse. When you realize the immense potential benefits, Unity is the only viable option.

Unity has costs and benefits that are consequential to being one with another. Consider the following example. The *Titanic*, a gigantic ocean liner, sank after hitting an iceberg. Women were first in line for the lifeboats, and then men, if there was room. A woman was in line for rescue, but her husband was not with her. Considering the reality of leaving him, she voluntarily left the line and went to stand with her husband—for certain death together.

That is the ultimate test of Unity. Your life is one with the life of your spouse. Our exemplar counted it a greater benefit to die with her husband than to live without him. As such, she was one with her spouse.

Imagine the emotions felt by the husband when he saw his wife leave the line and come to stand with him for certain death. Imagine the ensuing feelings as they tried to grapple with the ethics of the decision relating to children, family, and responsibilities. Would a loving husband want his wife to die *needlessly* with him? No matter if the wife returned to the lifeboat line or stood with her husband, the emotions would be overwhelming. Imagine the intense feelings of husband and wife waiting together for certain death by the most horrible means—asphyxiation by drowning. Their short finale in the Marital Dance must have been the ultimate of human emotions—voluntarily dying in Unity, as one.

There is a wide range of reactions to the above example, from disdain to admiration. Did the husband and wife act selfishly or in the noble confines of agape love? The above illustrates the wisdom of agape love in suggesting a course of action for a given set of circumstances. Given the time constraints, the uncertainty of events, and the intense overriding emotions, only the couple can decide how best to practice agape love.

The universal lesson from the above is that the virtues of Unity must be governed by agape love.

The *Titanic* example of Unity has roots in antiquity. A long time ago, a daughter-in-law powerfully expressed the dimensions of Unity to her mother-in-law. A variation of that expression of Unity is repeated at many wedding ceremonies:

> For where you go, I will go. Where you stay, I will stay. Your people shall be my people, and your God my God. Where you die, I will die, and there will I be buried. May only death part you and me.
>
> —Ruth 1:16–17

The above expresses the beautiful side of Unity: devotion and loyalty. In marital reality, many people experience a broken kind of Unity—they are united in name, but not enjoying the bond of Unity. When one partner consistently harms or poisons the marital body, those actions will strain the bond of Unity. The body will tolerate and be one with a painful arm that is temporarily below par. However, when the arm becomes destructive to the body, the arm must go. The beautiful side of Unity happens when each mate willingly accepts responsibilities and works toward the common good. Indeed, the beautiful side of Unity is magnified when governed by agape love.

There is another critical reality. Unity is impossible when a spousal combination is fundamentally incompatible, or the partners insist on maintaining their individuality. Water and oil do not mix; they result in no functional, unified whole. A loving person cannot be unified with a hateful person. Likewise, a person of faith cannot enjoy unity with an atheist. They may coexist; however, each will lose potential when harnessed together because they pull toward opposing goals.

The lesson: during courtship, look for a mate with whom Unity follows naturally. The overriding question during courtship should be "Am I willing to become one with this person, warts and all?" If the answer is neutral, proceed with caution. If the answer is negative, find a new dance partner. Attempts to change a person during the demands of the Marital Dance seldom work.

Before we became one, my wife and I agreed to conduct our marriage according to New Testament guidelines. My wife became one with me after saying, "I do." I also said, "I do," without appreciating the implications. Instead, I focused on the benefits my wife brought to me. Consequently, our relationship suffered because of my lack of understanding and application. As I wrote this book, the importance of Unity to the success of the marital relationship came into focus. When I made Unity a two-way street, my wife confirmed the positive changes in our relationship.

As of this writing, my wife and I have enjoyed more than sixty years together. At our age, we often joke that we had to become one to survive. For example, I asked my wife to help me get the rocking chair going. Fortunately, it is not that bad—yet. Regardless, we are bound as one in recognition of past benefits and present needs. We found that the higher our level of Unity, the higher our potential to enjoy an enduring Marital Dance.

The following is a personal example of the binding power of Unity. Calving season on our farm required contact with cow and calf. Usually, my children and I made that contact—until I had a heart attack during the height of calving season. The heart attack took me out of circulation. I recall one cold, rainy night when the temperature was near freezing—the worst of nights for calving. The cold, wet air sucked the life from the newborn calves, such that they required immediate shelter and attention. That night we had six calves and their mothers that needed personal care to make it through the night.

Though my wife was not fond of contact with animals, she and my daughter stepped up to the plate and did what had to be done, without complaint. That self-sacrifice under harsh conditions is the essence of Unity: for the benefit to all. When I was down and out, my wife demonstrated that she was one with me. Unity is the glue that binds a marital relationship when the going gets tough.

Think through the ramifications and benefits of being one with your spouse. Then ask, "What can we do to increase the strength of our unity bond?" To aid in that self-analysis, take the Marital Fitness Test detailed earlier in this book. Also, review the fourteen steps toward marital unity detailed in Chapter 7.

Be True

In the context of a happy marital relationship, how do you identify and correctly apply truth? Consider the following statement that appears to be universally true: for maximum benefit, a couple must pull in unison toward a common goal. As the photo shows, in some applications, it is best to work in opposition to your mate. Given that dichotomy, this section will concentrate on the importance of truth in a happy, enduring Marital Dance.

There is an overriding issue concerning the value of truth. The desired results are consequential to knowing and correctly applying truth. An expert marksperson will always miss the mark with a faulty weapon believed to be accurate (true). Likewise, a false premise faithfully applied will always miss its mark, providing less than the desired results. Simply, a happy marital relationship is nourished by truth correctly applied.

My parents were very religious, but they could not apply the truth of their faith to their marriage. As a result, they made life miserable for each other and the family. Each showed a face of distrust and dislike, resulting in a marriage that reflected their faces. To avoid their errors, my wife and I agreed to go by the truth in the Book. That truth helped put smiles on our faces and love in our hearts, which was reflected in our marriage.

The truth in the Book—how do two imperfect people practice those profound words? We were married for maybe a month when I came home to a crying wife. Since I couldn't find a section in the Book about soothing a crying wife, I was on my own. So I asked the obvious question: "What's wrong?" I thought that maybe she was crying because we had moved into a converted chicken coop on my folks' place (which we did).

Her answer was unexpected. Before we were married, I knew that my wife didn't play some games, such as tennis and chess, that I enjoyed. No matter, I thought. She could play her games with the girls, and I would play my games with the boys. As far as I knew, none of that violated the Book. The response from my wife indicated that I had missed a fundamental truth in the Book. She told me the rest of the story through tears flowing down her soft, lovely cheeks. She had moved away from her friends and family in California to be my wife in Ohio. In Ohio, she had no one but me, her new husband. That new husband was spending his evenings playing games with his friends. Per biblical truth, she wanted to be one with her husband, but her husband was still one with his friends.

Wow! That truth hit home hard, and I was unprepared. That was the only time I considered divorce, but only for a moment and never seriously. We had committed to each other for life; divorce was not an option. The only viable option was to fulfill my vow and become one with my wife, per biblical truth.

The practice of truth in all its forms is fundamental to a happy marital relationship. However, the quest for truth, the understanding of truth, the desire and discipline to correctly apply truth, and the will to pay the costs of truth can be challenging in a Marital Dance. The difficulties are nourished in a relationship in which your spouse's faults often butt against your personality defects.

The burden to know, discern, and practice truth is personal. "Each one should be fully convinced in his mind" (Rom 14:5 ESV). In a marital relationship, you and your spouse will make the final decisions that will govern your lives and your Marital Dance, for good or evil.

To help make truth-based decisions, apply a memory gem I learned in grade school (from Shakespeare's *Hamlet*).

This above all to thine own self be true, and it must follow as the night the day, thou canst not then be false to any man.

The motto for this book is a form of the same idea: I shall be true to God, to my spouse, and to myself. In abbreviated form and for emphasis: *we shall be true*.

To be *true* means to be steadfast, loyal, honest, just, consistent, and faithful.

You cannot be true outside the practice of truth.

The Origin of Truth

All biblical instructions and guidelines have their roots in the two Great Commandments (Mat 22:36–40). These commandments are the nutrients of the BBI. The Great Commandments are positive and dynamic in application: *do*, as in love.

For marital behavior, start with the BBI and then check against the Great Commandments. Behavioral truth is condensed into the Great Commandments. As suggested by the photo, burn these commandments into your mind for automatic recall and practice.

LOVE THE LORD, WITH ALL YOUR HEART, SOUL, AND MIND

AND

LOVE YOUR (SPOUSE) AS YOU LOVE YOURSELF

To some Christians, the phrase "to thine own self be true" promotes self, taking God out of the equation. I assert the contrary: the motto builds upon biblical admonishments to seek the truth, which has its origin in our Creator. Biblically, we are to "know the truth, and the truth shall make you free" (John 8:32). Since we are not the center of truth, we should seek it and act accordingly; that is the objective.

In marriage, two people who are different mentally, physically, and spiritually will share the same cocoon. The best insurance for a happy relationship in that cocoon is when those two differences share and act upon the same time-tested truth. To enjoy the ideal Marital Dance, know, act upon, and practice truth.

The foundational truth is that a harmonious, lifetime Marital Dance requires that husband and wife are compatible in values, traditions, behavior, ideals, faith, and so on. It follows that a harmonious Marital Dance is impossible if the husband and wife have divergent views on critical issues. For example, atheists and Christians cannot coexist in harmony since the truths of their core values conflict. The lesson is clear: ensure that you and your spouse share common truth in all critical areas. Make sure during the Courtship Dance; it is generally too late in the Marital Dance.

The difficulty is that truth is difficult to discern. Variations of truth have many faces formed by faith, people, books, TV, experience, tradition, and more. The faces of influence appear honorable and trustworthy. Yet they flood us with a divergent range of suggestions—often proclaimed as truth—on a wide variety of issues, including the Marital Dance. In each face of influence, there may be an element of truth. However, there is no universal understanding of and agreement about truth or what it means in application. Indeed, as the following photo suggests, sometimes it is difficult to discern truth even when you see it. That leads to the big question: How do you determine the face of truth from the face of fiction?

Photo: True or Fabricated?

The photo is authentic but appears to be fabricated. If the photo was not staged or altered, then what is its purpose? Where was it taken? What is the truth behind the photo? What is the message of the photo? Ask ten people, and you will get ten different answers. In such cases, there is only one way to know *the truth:*

go to the source, the photographer. Similarly, to know the truth relative to a joyful, endearing marriage, go to the Creator of the Marital Dance and reference the BBI of His Book, which tells how to ensure a joyful Marital Dance for life.

(The still-life photo was taken in the dining room of a river cruiser going through a lock.)

To frustrate the quest for truth, progressive thinking says, "There is no absolute moral truth except in this statement." Agreed, it is difficult to define truth for all occasions, for all people, and for all time. It is difficult to determine where the valley ends and the mountain begins. However, there is no controversy when deep in the valley or on the top of the mountain. Since the practice of truth is fundamental to a successful marriage, how can we recognize the face of time-proven truth from the myriad faces of partial truths paraded as the whole truth?

Most behaviors have nuance exceptions that are accepted in law and biblical context. The Bible and the law say that we should not kill. Yet, according to Old Testament scripture, God commanded His people to kill and destroy the enemy. The word *destroy* is used 212 times in the King James Version of the Old Testament. We should not be jealous, yet we are told, "Jehovah your God is a jealous God" (Deu 6:15).

To frustrate the quest for truth, words have a variety of meanings that make a statement of absolute behavior difficult or impossible to define. Nuanced situations exist in which some people will die if you do, and others will die if you do not. In such a case, it would be unjust to apply the commandment "You shall not kill" as an absolute.

So is there an absolute behavior that holds for all time in all situations? This is where the BBI of the New Testament shines with wisdom. The biblical answer to relative behavior is found in one of the verses quoted above. Can you find it?

To find the answer, let us start with some basics. Perhaps the most basic of fundamentals is that truth is noncontradictory for the same set of events at the same time and location. Given that reality, is the commandment "You shall not kill" (or murder) an absolute? Merriam Webster defines *murder* as "the unlawful killing of a person with malice aforethought." Even with that definition, it is difficult to write a law that holds for all nuanced cases. How can you determine with certainty whether a murderous act was committed with *malice aforethought*? Any murderous act has to have some forethought, but is that forethought necessarily malicious?

It seems hopeless. Guidelines, instructions, and rules have little merit since they are laced with myriad definitions and exceptions that negate their value. When a person is asked about what makes an enjoyable marriage, the answer is simplistic: "Do what you think is right and hope for the best."

The Bible has anticipated the above response and provided an absolute for all time and circumstances. Indeed, that absolute is the parent to all behaviors defined in the BBI. That is the essence of wisdom: to reduce the complex to the vital one. That vital one is agape love that takes the spotlight in the Great Commandments (Mat 22:36–40). Agape love is the mother of all the behaviors noted in the BBI. Under the umbrella of agape love, those behaviors can be practiced confidently toward a happy marital relationship.

Now, let's consider the ramifications.

Truth

Outside of truth, the above is no more than a family of words. So how do we know truth? Truth can be verified after it has been thoroughly time-tested, without error or conflicting results. Interestingly and significantly, the quality-based math to certify truth is exceptionally harsh. If you make only one or two tests with no errors, the (mathematical) confidence level is less than 50 percent that the test results are repeatable. To certify an unproven hypothesis, behavior, or whatever can require (dependent on history) up to two thousand error-free test periods to have a reasonable degree of certainty that the unproven will perform as desired. Accordingly, certifying an unproven, novel behavior in a lifetime is not possible. Those time-dependent realities are why the time-proven BBI are critical to a lasting marital relationship. You can confidently apply the BBI to achieve results that are repeatable and predictable.

Due to differences in people and circumstances, the results will vary. For example, smoking is deemed harmful for all. That harm can vary from minor to deadly. As such, our motto comes into play. In application, be true!

Truth Does Not Identify Itself

Truth in its many forms comes with many faces. Which of those faces is true or comes closest to the truth? Unfortunately, truth does not identify itself. Even worse, the faces of perceived truth can appear attractive and convincing, making it even more difficult to identify the true face from the fakes.

An ultimate (and maybe final) thrill would be jumping off a high cliff and doing aerial maneuvers on the way down. However, we do not jump off high cliffs because the feedback is immediate and harsh—intense pain and death. Unfortunately, most behaviors and decisions are not like that; they provide up-front highs without immediate feedback to guide our decision-making. For example, eating just one doughnut today feels good and has no adverse effects that we can tell. However, a doughnut a day for ten years adds up to 3,650 doughnuts that most likely will result in obesity and its negative impact.

Be true. The literature and the BBI abound with time-proven guidelines for health and relationship issues. You have only one little life, one Marital Dance. Be true, and practice accordingly.

Beware of Perceived Truths

The challenge: how can we identify the true face of truth in a vast field of faces, most of which are fakes? Toward an answer, let us review the nature of some of the faces of truth.

Partial truths, by definition, are not inclusive. In a marital relationship, partial truth interpreted as the whole truth can lead to tragic ends. For instance, on one occasion, while I was away from home on a business trip, my wife opened a letter addressed to me (a mutually agreed practice). In that letter was a fashion page with a photo of a model. On the photo, the model had written, "John, come see me anytime you are in the area."

To exacerbate the incident, we were having family problems. This article was about to be the straw that broke the camel's back. My wife's bastion of security had shown his colors, and they were not pretty.

What she saw and read was true, but outside of context, it was partial truth. Based on the photo and note, my wife assumed I was doing illicit business while away from home. That resulted in unkind thoughts new to her. Fortunately, before any lasting damage was done, she recognized the model's name, revealing the truth. The model was a distant relative and not a "second mate."

Another example of partial truth is tragically common in the Christian community. Typically, that partial truth is expressed as a variation of "Just trust in the Lord and all will be OK." First, that statement ignores the realities of cause-and-effect behavior. The high divorce rate in the Christian community shows that something is wrong with that statement, how it is understood, or its application. Perhaps the greatest misapplication is in the word *trust*. In many cases, we trust the Lord to do for us, but we don't trust Him sufficiently to know and practice His truth and instructions.

Remember, effects are built into and consequential to the behavior. If you get a divorce, go deeply into debt, or commit adultery, God and family can forgive, but the action remains. The deed is done. It comes with consequences, and it will demand its due. You will pay.

Circumstantial truths depend upon conditions and context. Potential evil results when beneficial behavior fades into destructive behavior. Beneficial behavior taken to excess can be ruinous: food, TV, movies, clothing, language, rest, and even prayer and Bible study that are out of balance with critical needs can cause harm.

Some people believe you can't pray or study the Bible too much. Maybe so, but consider the following two examples that challenge that statement as circumstantial and not the whole truth.

With her family gone, my mother had no way to get to church. After a year or so of not attending, she received a visit from her pastor. The pastor was not long in the house when he noted some beer cans and questioned my mother about them. The questions were stern, since the church took a firm stand against strong drink.

My mother was not one to let a monkey on her back. She quickly explained that she couldn't sleep at night, so her son-in-law had brought her a six-pack of beer and suggested she try a can before going to bed. She did, and it helped her sleep. She then put the monkey on the pastor's back. "You had many prayer meetings over the past year. You had time to pray but had no time to visit a widow or offer help. Yet when I took a can of beer that helped me sleep, you, who did nothing but pray, criticized that which helped."

This is not to condone or condemn drinking. It is only to say that the good (prayer and Bible study) can fade into harm and even evil (neglect of duty) if one is not careful to keep life balanced. That potential fading of good into evil is especially true of strong drink—a reason I don't buy or have it in the house. Because of individual strengths and weaknesses, what is true for you may not be true for me and vice versa.

The other example is tragic. Unfortunately, it is common among many Christians who conscientiously raise their children "the Bible way." Yet their children live outside the faith in apparent contradiction of the biblical truth recorded in Proverbs 22:6: "Train up a child in the way he should go: and when he is old, he will not depart from it."

My wife and I attended a faith-based conference. One of the main speakers gave a powerful sermon on Proverbs 22:6. His conclusion: if the parents regularly have family devotions, their children will not go astray, as biblically promised.

Then came the unexpected. The next speaker, emphatically but kindly, refuted the previous speaker's conclusions. Based on his experience as a youth counselor, he noted that many of his problem youth were drowning in biblical theology, history, and commands. These youth did not have a balanced view of God or their parents. They knew about God and their parents but didn't enjoy a personal relationship with either. The desired personal relationship to guide their daily actions was missing. Living out of balance, these youth were gasping for life-sustaining air. Accordingly, they did not experience the promised joys of their faith and wanted out. Their circumstantial truths were out of balance with realities.

False truths, perceived as the whole truth, can be destructive or even deadly. In the Marital Dance, it can be (very) difficult to identify false truth that appears innocent, enjoyable, and without consequences. Examples are the arguments for "safe sex" outside of marriage: "Since sex is natural and normal, do it and enjoy." Similarly, many new, unproven trends relative to family structures suggest caution (for noncritical issues) to avoidance (for critical issues) until we have time-proven results.

In some cases, truth for one is falsity for another. For example, the statement "Peanut butter is a nutritious food" is true for some and false, even deadly, for others. People who have an allergy to peanuts can die from ingesting even a tiny amount. Similarly, the concept of safe sex has many faces, from the procreation of life to the destruction of life.

The above realities take us back to our motto: be true. Know yourself, know God's plan (the BBI), and be sure. If in doubt, for decisions with significant ramifications as in marriage: *don't.*

Misapplied truths generally result in less than the desired results. In some cases, truth misapplied can be worse than truth ignored. In a marital dispute, we can fuel the fire by letting our emotions dictate our responses. In that case, doing nothing is the better option.

Generally, we will not experience the desired results in a marital relationship if we fail to know or correctly apply the time-proven BBI. The resulting failures may have compounding effects. Due to misapplication, the results will be less than desired. A typical reaction to failure is to place blame. The misapplied BBI are perceived to be out of touch with present-day realities. As such, we can dig ourselves into the mire by faulty reasoning and faulty application of the tried-and-true BBI.

Truth: A Six-Legged Horse?

Sometimes truth has conflicting faces, as suggested by the unaltered photo above. At first, you will see only three legs, then four, five, and finally six legs on the horse. Except for possible genetic anomalies, horses have four legs. The photo suggests that when making critical decisions, we should not rely on a single piece of evidence that may hide or distort the truth. Additional views may reveal what is lost in a single viewpoint. When making critical decisions, be true. Be sure.

The photo poses the question and provides the answer to the question. As with many truths, the whole truth of the image may be difficult to discern. With regard to truth, seek and you shall find. The truth of the photo is that a second horse is behind the one you see.

Relative to a marital relationship, you and your spouse may see the same picture but come to different conclusions. You may see your family auto on its last leg, calling for a replacement. Your spouse may see the family car with many service miles left, its replacement less urgent than saving toward a down payment on a house.

Biblically, the husband makes the final decision after considering his mate's desires and input. Ideally, the final decision is in line with biblical truth and with what is best for the family.

To discern the truth for difficult choices, my wife and I resorted to the decision-making process described as Insurance Measure 4 in Chapter 5. For most decisions, we were able to agree by applying the following three guidelines:

- Is the decision (procedure, principle, or behavior) supported by time-proven results?
- Does the decision build upon and support other time-proven precepts?
- Does the behavior or decision conform to the time-proven BBI?

If the answer to any of the above was negative, we looked for a better solution.

From a Christian perspective, it appears holy, right, and easy to step back and let God, rather than to step up to the plate and play by His rules and regulations.

Now Make it Happen:

To enjoy Life to the Max,
   Do the Marital Dance Magnificently.
To Dance Magnificently,
   Make sure that your Practice of the BBI is TRUE.

Truth applied

Since we are different, we should not pattern our lives after others who live in different environments and have different values, strengths, and weaknesses. In marriage, we should ensure that our objectives, realities, strengths, and weaknesses are tuned to the truths of the BBI.

In personal and marital decision-making:

Don't Ask "What is wrong with…?"

If you search long enough, you can find a nuanced rationale to justify any behavior. For example, "What is wrong with smoking?"

> The Bible doesn't say that smoking is wrong.
> My grandpa lived until he was ninety-one; smoking didn't hurt him.

Or consider the argument some make about sex outside of marriage: "A bad tree does not bear good fruit. Premarital sex cannot be wrong when the result is the 'good fruit' of a beautiful, innocent child."

Such arguments are shallow, not the whole truth. The whole truth includes the net long-term effects, which can be harmful and deadly.

Instead ask, "Is there a better way?"

Why settle for less than the best?

There is a caveat: if we are not disciplined, we can allow our emotions to override reason. An emotional response can provide immediate gratification, whereas reason typically has up-front costs for delayed benefits. Decisions that are emotionally driven can often result in long-term harm. A tragic example is King Solomon of the Bible, who wrote the book of Proverbs that he applied to all but himself. In time, he and his nation suffered the consequences—because Solomon was not true to his God-given gift of wisdom.

To help ensure that you follow reason over emotion, assume that you have a revolver pointed at your head. You know it will do its horrible thing *if* you allow emotion to rule over reason—over truth. Since behavior is a matter of cause and effect, there is symbolically a revolver pointed at your head that will ensure the consequences of misbehavior. To live and enjoy, behave accordingly.

Make it central to your thinking. Your behavior is fundamental to an enjoyable, lifetime Marital Dance. Your behavior is a cause with built-in effects—for good or evil, for blessings or painful consequences

In your quest to enjoy, *be true* and *be sure*.

Limits

Some marital issues, such as emotional disorders, addiction, and the like, can be extremely complex. These require specialized expertise outside the scope of this book.

A book can't focus on and adjust to each person's unique characteristics and needs. Accordingly, take what fits and modify it to your bent, or ignore it and move on.

It is your life: be sure by being grounded in truth.

Chapter 2
The Courtship and Marital Dances

How shall we dance? Answers to that question come from various sources, all claiming to be the ultimate. So how do you decide, and what is the basis for your decision? Toward an answer, we will review the advantages and disadvantages of the two most prominent models for the Marital Dance: the Secular Model followed by the Biblical Model.

The Secular Model

Variations of the Secular Model have their roots in antiquity. The current model is politically correct and accepted by most as the standard for marital conduct.

The Secular Model for the Marital Dance is brief and straightforward: *50/50* and *100/100*. In application, each partner has equal say (50 percent), and each should give 100 percent to bring out the beauty and grace of the Marital Dance. On the first pass, the Secular Model appears brilliant in its simplicity and merit. Let's apply it and see what happens.

In application, the Secular Model has no prescribed music to set the tempo, no designed leadership to guide the dance, and no choreography for the ethics of the Courtship or Marital Dances. In application, the Marital Dance is whatever the dancers make it. No rules, no guidelines, and no detail are required to ensure a beautiful, graceful, enduring dance. Even worse, there are no guidelines to determine or define your 50 percent say in decision-making or when you have reached your 100 percent contribution. In a dispute, there is no way to measure your 50 percent or 100 percent contribution versus that of your mate.

Consequently, in the Secular Model, an inept dancer with 50 percent rights has equal say with a good dancer, who is also limited to 50 percent. In making critical decisions in a marital relationship, whose 50 percent wins? If the dance partners are each sure they are right and give it 100 percent, the resulting dance will be a disaster—a reason for divorce.

To appreciate the negative ramifications, consider a basketball team with a coach who keeps it simple: a) all are equal with equal say, and b) all are expected to give 100 percent. The basics sound good, but how do you play the game without rules?

The Secular Model looks good and has some merit; however, it is incomplete and unworkable when applied. It results in a Marital Dance by chance. Results confirm the above conclusions. Since the Christian community adopted variations of the Secular Model, the Christian divorce rate (failure rate) has been about the same as that of the secularists.

The Biblical Model

The Biblical Model, detailed in the BBI, likewise appears brilliant in its simplicity. Let's put it to the test.

The Biblical Model defines three essentials for a lifetime Marital Dance: the music (agape love), the choreography, and the behavior of husband and wife. The basics of marital behavior are summarized below (from Eph 5:21–33; 1 Pet 3:1–7; Col 3:18–19; 1 Cor 13).

> Husbands, love your wives as Christ loved the church and gave his life for it.
> Love your wives as you love yourselves, your bodies.
> Wives, submit yourselves to your husbands.
> Respect and support your husbands.
> The two shall become as one flesh and mutually submit to one another.

Note that the Biblical Model reduces to a three-step program designed to ensure an enduring Marital Dance. Unity in the ultimate is defined as one flesh in mutual submission. In Unity, superiority of the husband or wife is impossible. A husband or wife who assumes dominance or superiority in the marital relationship does so outside the Biblical Model.

The husband is responsible for leading the Marital Dance according to the will of God. However, the wills of both husband and wife are subject to the will of God. In that sense, the Marital Dance is similar to a square dance, in which the couple dances to the leadership of the caller. In the Marital Dance, the *caller* is the Creator who wrote the music and inspired the choreography described in the BBI.

The wife willingly submits to and follows the lead of her husband. The wife submits, knowing that her husband's will reflects the will of God. She also knows that her interests are secured by her husband's life if need be. Accordingly, the biblical plan provides *support* for the husband, *security* for the wife, and the *benefits* of Unity for both.

Note that the Biblical Model includes, but is not limited to, the 50/50 and the 100/100 of the Secular Model. The Biblical Model destroys any basis for superiority by declaring husband and wife as one. The Biblical Model secures the 100/100 to the max; the husband's 100 percent includes giving his life for his wife. The wife provides 100 percent support to her husband's leadership.

In application, I can't imagine a more equitable, simple, and practical plan to ensure a complex relationship for the benefit of all

Caution: The validity of the Biblical Model is critically dependent upon the faithful practice of the BBI by both husband and wife.

The Troublesome Biblical Model

We know that cultures change, bringing in new concepts and challenges. The Secular Model is designed to fit the present culture. It may have shortcomings, but it is politically correct. In contrast, the Biblical Model is defined by terms such as *leader, follower,* and *submission*. To many, these terms are unacceptable, troublesome, and politically incorrect—reasons for rejection.

In response, consider that the traditional dances, such as the waltz, require a follower who willingly submits to and supports the leader. There is no superiority in that relationship, only responsibility. When one observes the beautiful, graceful waltz, Unity stands out with no hint of dominance, superiority, or control.

Sometimes the follower will be a better dancer than the leader. In that case, a wise leader will learn from and incorporate the ways of the follower.

Unacceptable

I recall an editorial in the *Wall Street Journal* that mocked the Biblical Model for its (apparent) emphasis on male superiority and dominance in the marital relationship. Similarly, a neighbor heard in the news that the

Baptists were encouraging marriage per biblical instruction. According to the article, the Baptists put the wife in a servant role to the husband. My neighbor gave up her Baptist membership until she learned the rest of the story.

So let us concentrate on the rest of the story as told in the BBI. The husband has the responsibility to lead in the Marital Dance within the guidelines established by the exemplary leadership of Christ. The biblical net for the husband's leadership is service unto death for his spouse if needed. That reality is the antithesis of the leadership described by the media.

In explaining the disparity, the newspaper stories concentrated on a piece of the puzzle and ignored the total picture. It is like defining a rosebush by focusing on the thorns and ignoring the blossoms. Marriage can easily be destroyed when a partial truth is perceived as the whole truth.

Not only did the media have it wrong, but it had nothing better to offer. It does not take much intelligence to throw sticks and stones. However, it takes disciplined and structured intelligence to build with sticks and stones.

Synergy

If performed biblically to the classical music of agape love, the Marital Dance provides an unexpected benefit: *synergistic gain* for both husband and wife. So what is synergy?

Synergy is a combination that results in a total greater than the sum of the parts. For example, on a single bike, my wife usually required fifty minutes to complete a hilly, nine-mile, circular route, compared to my forty-four minutes. On a tandem bike (a bike built for two), we should do the circular route in forty-seven minutes $[(50 + 44)/2 = 47]$. However, by working together, we covered that route in about forty minutes. Together, we beat my wife's best time by ten minutes, my best time by four minutes, and the average by seven minutes. That reality, called *synergy,* leads to the objective and beauty of the Courtship Dance—to find a mate with whom the synergistic gain exceeds individual potential.

Personal experience confirms the above. I am a more disciplined person when bonded as one with my wife. Because of the synergistic gain, my wife and I are more financially secure than our single or divorced peers. With some couples, the positive synergistic effects are dramatic, involving significant shifts in personality, lifestyle, and the like. From observation of family and friends, happily married couples outperform their single peers in health and economics.

When a marital couple retains their independent airs, the synergy can go negative and even become destructive, the total being less than the sum of the individual parts. For example, my mother and father were talented and disciplined. Unfortunately, they used their talents toward mutual destruction. My mother was lethal with her talent of self-preservation honed to perfection through war and revolution. She would do her duty—in her way—but she would not support and be submissive to a man who did not or could not support her needs, let alone her wants. Consequently, my father could not lead in the Marital Dance, which resulted in additional avalanches of rebuke from my mother. My father also had an old-world mindset: father and husband held absolute authority. As such, my father generally acted independently of my mother's needs or desires. By maintaining their independent airs, my parents ensured they would never enjoy what they wanted—a Marital Dance of grace, beauty, and harmony.

Confirmation

The all-important question is this: Does the Biblical Model produce the desired results? The results will confirm or falsify the question.

Before our marriage, my wife and I agreed that the Bible would define our marital relationship. Per biblical guidance, would I give my life to protect hers? An experience in the Boundary Waters Canoe Area provided the *bare* answer. A *bear* invaded our camp to find the source of the Canadian bacon odor. I instinctively put myself between the bear and my wife. She now knows her value to me.

The skeptic may still demand: "OK, show how you biblically resolved a critical issue that could have potentially divided you."

Fair enough. Here is such an issue. While driving home from our daughter's house, about five hours away, my wife put our marital commitment to the test. She wanted to be near and enjoy family life with our daughter. However, she also made it clear that she was one with me regardless of my decision. She said no more—no threats, no consequences—simply, "This is what I desire, but my ultimate desire is to be with you, whether here or there."

My wife's presentation of her desire was honed to biblical perfection. I had to respond in kind. There was no viable compromise; we could relocate or stay. By mutual agreement, I had to make the critical decision.

To exacerbate the decision-making, I was recovering from triple-bypass heart surgery. Moving would entail stress. We had lived on our farm for seventeen years. That farm reflected our character. We had raised our children on that farm, and family memories were born on that farm. Our beautiful, homey, hillside farm overlooked the elegant Seneca Lake. The farm was rich in mineral rights that proved very valuable with the advent of fracking for oil. The farm was home.

Given the above, my preference was to stay. However, our premarital agreement said I would give her needs and desires equal or greater value than mine. The move was important to her, but how important? To be sure, I had to find my wife's inner desire.

So, I asked her: "How important is the move to you? Fifty-fifty means you can stay or move; it doesn't matter much. Sixty-forty means you would rather move, but staying is not that bad." I was ready to say more, but she had the drift.

"If that is what you mean, the answer is ninety-ten."

Since my answer to that question was forty-sixty, I had no choice but to honor her request. Her response showed that the move was essential to her happiness and well-being. We now have a cozy and comfortable home less than a mile from our daughter's home. Another positive: thirty years after the surgery, my heart is still going strong.

In contrast, note that the Secular Model has no means to resolve a no-compromise, emotionally driven issue. Although the "50/50 and 100/100" basics of the Secular Model have merit, there is no procedure to make a good decision.

Summary

The basics of enjoying synergistic gain from the Biblical Marital Dance are simple.

- **The husband and wife become one flesh**
    by melding each other's needs, desires, and capabilities.
- **The husband's commitment to his wife is ultimate,**
    secured by his life if need be.
- **With that ultimate security, the wife submits**
    and supports the leadership of her husband.
- **The two become one in Christ.**
- **Consequently, they dance as one**
    to the music of agape love
    and to the choreography prescribed by the BBI.

Chapter 3
Marital Basics

Ensuring a beautiful, graceful Courtship Dance requires that the dance music, choreography, and dancers all be true to their prescribed roles. The lifetime Marital Dance has another critical requirement. In addition to the music and choreography, the dancers must be compatible with basic values and behavior, since they will share the same cocoon for life. Accordingly, the marital basics relate to the music, choreography, skills, and behavior of the dancers (husband and wife).

The Music

In traditional dance, the music doesn't tell the dancers what to do; instead, the music suggests the movements. Likewise, in our symbolic Marital Dance, we need music to guide each dancer's movements and behavior. Symbolically, *love is the music* for the Marital Dance. Love does not dictate an action; it suggests an action to maintain and enhance a relationship. For the Marital Dance, the forms of music are *eros, agape,* and *tough love.*

The following photo illustrates the distinctive line that separates eros from agape love. Eros love feeds on the external, as by the winsome face of the. caterpillar In time, the reality of the persona of the caterpillar takes center stage. That is when Eros love fades, and agape love shows its face. Emotions fuel eros love. Agape love is fueled by the total person—the lovable traits and warts. Even though we may not like a person (we find their ways unappealing), agape love always answers the question in the photo in the affirmative.

Do You Love Me
Or do you Not?

It seems that I Forgot.

Eros Love

The Greek word *eros* relates to romantic love that is sexually and emotionally stimulated and driven. Eros love is the magnetism that attracts male and female. Generally, it is at its strongest during the courtship and early stages of the marital relationship. In the early stages, the love relationship is readily advertised, as suggested in the following photo. If not nurtured, the emotionally driven eros love can fade and even go negative, resulting in coexistence, divorce, and death in the extreme.

I know of three cases in which eros love ended in death. The most tragic case involved a young man whom I will call Rodger. Rodger seemed solid, with a pending engineering degree from a local university. He was in love with a young woman who, while dating Rodger, found Rodger's friend more attractive. In response, negative eros love adrenalized Rodger and took control of his emotions, which overrode reason. Rodger shot and killed his ex-girlfriend and her new boyfriend—his past friend. After those horrific acts, Rodger turned the revolver to his head and pulled the trigger. That was his last act.

In another case, I was promoted to a position left empty by the suicide of a fellow employee whose wife was unfaithful.. The third case involved a double murder over a stalled love affair.

Unfortunately, TV and history books are full of similar tragic incidents triggered by eros love gone sour. Fortunately, there is an answer to the reality of fading eros love and its potential evils. That answer is agape love, which shows its influence when your marital partner is less than lovely. So what is this magic force called agape love?

Agape Love

Agape is the pure form of love with both Latin and Greek roots. Agape love is a form of grace that shows interest in and responds to your spouse's critical needs, independent of worth or appeal. Agape love comes from a pure heart, a clear conscience, and a genuine faith (1 Tim 1:5 GNB).

For general application, agape love is the genius of the BBI. There is no way to write a code of behavior that will fit all cases. Enter agape love, which covers all the nuances of behavior. For nuance cases, agape love provides guidelines for an optimum response from a pure heart. A person cannot act with higher honor than in the spirit of agape love—even when hindsight shows a better alternative.

As the photo below suggests, a baby bird owes its life to its mother's agape love, which shows its merit to the lovely and unlovely. Agape love is defined in the so-called Love Chapter of 1 Corinthians 13, a masterpiece by Apostle Paul. Agape love is the glue that holds a marital relationship together for all but the extreme cases involving mental, physical, and spiritual disorders. Like traditional dance music, the rhythm and beat of agape love music suggest the movement, the action, and the response.

Because of agape love, I live

When you feel the music, the dance steps flow naturally. Accordingly, we want to feel and absorb the nature of agape love music toward automatic, intuitive application. So let us review the basics of agape love music as recorded in the Love Chapter.

I will make every effort to be the mate who—
- **is faithful and kind;**
- **feels and suffers the pain of my spouse;**
- **is not jealous of my spouse's accomplishments;**
- **does not feel superior;**
- **behaves appropriately;**
- **does not insist on my way;**
- **does not gloat over the faults of my spouse;**
- **is slow to anger and does not imagine evil of my spouse;**
- **encourages my spouse to practice the right;**
- **shares with, believes in, hopes in, and endures with my spouse; and**
- **proves my faith by loving my spouse when they are unlovely.**

In a happy, lasting marriage, the objective is to enjoy the benefits of both eros and agape love. Eros-agape love indicates a romantic, caring love for one's spouse that is hormone-driven and fueled by a faith-based spirit. Eros-agape love is perhaps the most valuable gift we can give to our spouses. It is the consummation and perfection of practiced grace. A marriage maintained by eros-agape love is about as good as it can be. No reasonable person would terminate a Marital Dance if their spouse gracefully dances to the music of eros-agape love. Your (our) objective is to be that spouse!

Sometimes a spouse faithfully practices eros-agape love, but their mate is not reciprocating. This can erode agape love to its limits. When agape love reaches its limits, enter tough love.

Tough Love

Tough love is a special case of agape love. Tough love is taking action for the good of a person (your mate) under the ethics and guidelines of agape love. You might say that tough love is agape love applied to difficult and trying people (you or your mate).

Perhaps the most challenging area of Christian behavior is our relationships with others. The interpersonal difficulties compound when the person out of control is your mate, whom you promised to love regardless. Since you will bear some consequences, your mate's misdeeds take on personal ramifications. How can a person effectively relate to their mate who is involved in a destructive lifestyle or is rejecting commonly held core values? How can you connect and be unified with a mate who squanders resources? How do you balance personal needs against their needs?

The objective in such situations is to effect positive changes in your mate. Even more troubling, what if you are the wayward mate? There are no easy answers. In all cases, the best solution starts with agape love that shows itself in forgiveness and change. After agape love, tough love takes over.

To illustrate, assume that your spouse loses it. In response, warn them. If the warning fails and your mate continues to be physical, abusive, or irresponsible, apply tough love. Do what needs to be done for the good of all. In extreme cases, you may have to leave your mate, but keep the door open for reconciliation (when your mate is repentant and takes corrective measures).

Sometimes we are the source of the problem. Other times, because of mental illness, addiction, and other reasons, the wisdom of God will be required to know when and how to practice tough love effectively. To ensure that tough love is appropriately applied, test against the ethic of agape love. Seek counsel from those you respect. For extreme cases, seek professional help. In some cases, the practice of love in all its wondrous forms reaches its limits. When those limits are reached, and you have done all you can, the Bible advises dusting yourself off and moving on to worthwhile endeavors (see Mat 10:14).

The objective is to effect positive change in yourself and your mate. There are no easy answers. Again, the magic elixir is agape love, which shows itself in repentance, forgiveness, and change.

Caution: the practice of tough love is perhaps the most difficult to effectively apply. Christians, parents, and authority figures are not necessarily sources of wisdom, ethics, or virtue. Always test against New Testament guidelines and instructions. Remember, the Bible makes exceptions. For example, we should keep the Sabbath day holy (no work) under normal circumstances. However, if the house is on fire or the ox is in the well, do not wait until tomorrow to act (Luke 13:10ff, 14:2ff). In all cases, *be sure* and *be true!*

Thoughts for Consideration
- A graceful Marital Dance is ensured when both partners perform to the music of eros-agape love. In all divorces and marital conflicts observed, one or both spouses did not practice agape love.
- Your response to the unlovely side of your spouse will be a measure of your mastery of agape love.
- Agape love is automatic, natural, and intuitive. .
- If the Marital Dance seems slow or tedious, you probably are not dancing in unity to the music of eros-agape love.

The Choreography

Choreography describes the composition, routine, and mechanics of a dance. Each type of dance has its unique choreography. A beautiful, graceful Marital Dance requires that both husband and wife are proficient in the time-tested choreography as defined in the BBI.

The Marital Dance starts with the traditional "I do" and ends when death is the parting gate. During marriage, the dancers' behavior becomes paramount and, in time, defines the choreography, according to which each must adjust to their spouse's behavior. This leads to the next section on cause-and-effect behavior.

Cause and Effect Behavior

The Overriding Issue: All Behavior Is Cause and Effect for Good or Evil

That statement seems to have its limits. Certainly, a baby bird (as in the photo below) cannot effect good or evil results. The photo poses the question and dramatically provides the answer in stark terms. The mind of the little bird thinks of food, and its mouth behaves accordingly—open for life and closed for certain death.

Likewise, in a marital relationship, our behavior is often defined by what we think and make public by way of our mouths. The open mouth that expresses love can also spit out venom that destroys a relationship. To enjoy the positive benefits, keep in mind that all behavior is a cause with consequential effects that are certain and apply to all—saint and sinner. Control your mind and mouth accordingly.

An Open Mouth: Cause for Good and Evil Effects

Unfortunately, the realities of cause-and-effect behavior are easily ignored. In the secular maxim, it's "Do your thing and enjoy." In many religious circles, the grace of God is given center stage with little to no emphasis on living the *ways of God*. For incentive to apply, the ways of God have sewn-in blessings and consequences. When the effects of misbehavior come into play, the response is "God, where were You? I trusted You. Why did You let this happen to me?"

It is not my intent to get into the theology of grace and its nuances. My intent is to say that all behavior has built-in consequences. Harsh words, infidelity, and the like can be forgiven; however, God cannot undo them once they are done.

Generally, behavior is a choice. For ultimate thrills, we can choose to jump off high places. During the fall, we can enjoy freedom of motion as in levitation; we can twist, turn, and glide all without effort—until we experience the sudden stop at the end of the fall. Every time we jump, we can count on the force of gravity to do its thing, and we can count on earth to ensure the consequential, sudden stop. Note that the mind defines the behavior; the physics of the behavior define the consequence.

Toward ensuring an enjoyable Marital Dance, we should practice that behavior with the desired, consequential effects. The problem: behavior does not come labeled as good or evil. Further, some behaviors have devastating effects far removed in time from the cause(s). So how can we know and behave toward enjoying a lifetime Marital Dance?

Fortunately, we do not have to experiment and suffer the painful effects of faulty behavior. Our Creator knows the hidden impacts of behavioral nuances. Accordingly, He lists those behaviors we should practice and those we should avoid. If we comply, we will enjoy the benefits consequential to that behavior. If we don't comply, the sudden stop at the end of the fall will let us know. In extreme cases, the fall can be fatal to a marital relationship.

Of significance to practice, the BBI are not God's arbitrary and capricious dictates: "Do as I say or else." Rather, they are God's listing of behaviors defined for our benefit: "Do these and enjoy; don't do those, for they can do you harm." As such, eagerly know and practice His ways toward an enjoyable, lifetime Marital Dance.

In a marital relationship, the results of cause-and-effect behavior are magnified—for good and evil. If the mates behave, they will enjoy the compounded effects of their behavior. Likewise, if they misbehave, they will experience compounded adversities. Worse, they will most likely blame their mate for the misfortunes. Indeed, the seeds for divorce are sown when a mate has to bear the costs, real or perceived, of their spouse's misbehavior.

To illustrate the pluses and minuses of behavior, let us review some prominent examples. To start, consider David of the Old Testament. Even though he was proclaimed "to be a man after My [God's] own heart" (Act 13:22), David let his emotions rule. The results were dishonorable relations with Bathsheba and shameful behavior by sending Bathsheba's husband, Uriah, to his death. After being found out, David made a classic prayer of repentance in Psalm 51.

Though forgiven, David's illicit acts were a done deal for all to review—forever. Some three thousand years later, David's reputation is still tarnished by the names Uriah and Bathsheba. The effects of his behavior also adversely affected his family and his nation. It would be difficult to respect and trust a mate who performed so shamefully and repented only after his acts were disclosed.

Similarly, consider Bill Clinton, who generally was a good president—until his affair with Monica. He later expressed regret. Even if God and his family forgave him, his legacy was tarnished by his infidelity and related denials. The scar from cause-and-effect behavior is permanent. Consider the effect on his wife. She may have forgiven, but her memory is likewise forever scarred.

To appreciate the long-range impacts of misbehavior, study the above examples for their hidden consequences. Imagine that you are David or Mr. Clinton. By most measures, you are a good leader. However, after your grievous affair, you have an albatross about your neck that will forever blemish your character and integrity. Add to those negatives the loss of respect from your children and those who trusted you. The effects of emotions out of control override your credentials.

Similarly, the tongue out of control can be like the piercing of the sword, "but the tongue of the wise heals" (Pro 12:18). Wisdom suggests that you taste your words for palatability before you spit them out. To ensure that words of comfort and peace are born in your mouth, run them through the sieve of agape love before you say them.

To illustrate the above, consider "The First Settler's Story." In this poetic presentation, the settler goes into the wilderness with his young wife to start a new life. On one fateful day, all goes wrong. In response, the settler vents his anger on his wife with harsh, biting words, saying she lies around and lets him do all the work. The settler immediately sees the cold, dark poison in his words and desires to pull them back, but he can't. His spoken venom leaves its evil mark on his beloved wife.

As so often happens, one bad event leads to another. In response to her husband's harsh words, the settler's wife sets out to find a lost cow. Faithfully she looks, going ever deeper into the unknown wilderness. Then a terrible summer squall hits. The settler comes home to an empty house and spends the night looking for his wife. Early in the morning, he returns to his cabin to find the door barely open. His heart leaps for joy, for his love has made it home. Yes, she has come and gone. She lies lifeless, not far from where he killed her with his tongue.

Note that the settler's experience dramatically illustrates cause-and-effect behavior and its potential evil to a marital relationship.

> And wheresoe'er this story's voice can reach,
> > This is the sermon I would have it preach:
> Boys flying kites haul in their white-winged birds;
> > You can't do that when you are flying words.
> "Careful with fire" is good advice we know;
> > "Careful with words" is ten times doubly so.
> Thoughts unexpressed can sometimes fall back dead,
> > But God Himself can't kill them once they're said.
> > > —Will Carleton

The lesson is there for those who will learn. From another perspective, the most beautiful love song results when both mates sing, behave, and dance in unison to the music of agape love.

In the following sections, I will review the cause-and-effect relationship in three different responses to the biblical narrative. The anecdotes are drawn from memory.

The Neanderthal Man

A husband and wife were professionals with related comforts. They practiced a variation of the secular dance model in which they each gave 100 percent and shared 50/50 in decision-making. Though they enjoyed a comfortable life, something was missing.

One day, the husband told his wife that he wanted more from marriage than just sharing a house. He had nothing against his wife, but he wanted out of their sterile relationship. Consequently, he asked for a divorce.

His wife was satisfied with their marriage. She didn't want to terminate the relationship permanently in divorce. So she asked for a month to think it over. The husband agreed.

The wife knew that staying the course was not an option, but what did her husband want? How could she satisfy an undefined want or need in her husband? Nothing came to her mind that seemed reasonable—well, almost nothing. She did remember a sermon given by her friend's pastor. That sermon laid out the biblical responsibilities of husband and wife in a marital relationship. The pastor's views were so primitive that she labeled him the *Neanderthal Man*.

With no other viable option, she decided to take the advice of the Neanderthal Man. That sermon, so out of reason, was burned into her mind. She would give it her best, partly out of curiosity, but mostly out of necessity. For at least a month, she practiced the biblical ways described by the Neanderthal Man.

To the Legal Limits

A woman went to her lawyer to file for divorce. She noted to the lawyer that her husband had hurt her. For payback, she wanted to cause him pain to the limits of the law. "I mean, I want to hurt him. I want to see him suffer. I want him to beg for mercy."

Intrigued and challenged by that unusual request, the lawyer asked her to come back the next day for his answer.

The next day, she returned to a beaming lawyer. "I have your answer. Traditional divorces have it wrong. We can skin your husband of all he is worth and more. However, in so doing, you will become the evil one. What we want to do is just the opposite. You know your husband, what he likes and dislikes. Do all you can to be the wife of his dreams. Then, when he is ready to die for you, let him have it with both barrels. Arrange a surprise candlelight dinner with his favorite foods prepared to gourmet perfection. Play soft, romantic background music. Dress in your finest and show your most pleasing personality. When he is in a total state of ecstasy, hand him the gift-wrapped divorce papers I have prepared for you. Give him the documents, and then, with a triumphant smile, walk out."

Her response was ecstatic: "I love it, I love it, I love it! I cannot wait to play the charade and see his face after handing him the divorce papers."

A Matter of Life and Death

A farmer's wife finally managed to get her ailing husband to see their family doctor. After examining the farmer, the doctor called the farmer's wife into his office and laid down the facts, starting with the bad news. "Unless your husband regains his desire to live, he will die within a year. However, there is hope if you can give him the will to live. Indulge him with his favorite food and snacks. After he comes in from work, bite your tongue if he gets out of sorts. Give him every attention." The doctor made several more suggestions. He then wished the wife good luck.

Now for the Rest of the Stories

A news commentator would tell a story with an open ending. He would close the anecdote with the traditional phrase "And now for the rest of the story." The rest of the story usually had a surprise ending. So let's find out the rest of the stories of the above anecdotes.

The wife in the first story was desperate to save her marriage. She faithfully applied the biblical marital instructions taught by the Neanderthal Man. After the trial month passed, she asked her husband about his divorce request. He replied, "I don't know what happened, but you became my ideal wife." In her words, her husband became her ideal.

As for the second story, after several months, the curious lawyer called the vengeance-seeking wife and asked how her husband took the divorce papers. She responded, "I never gave him the divorce papers. During the trial month, he made dramatic changes to become the mate of my dreams. No way would I divorce him now."

On the way home, the farmer in the third story asked his wife what the doctor had told her. Given the realities of the doctor's suggestion, the wife's answer was simple and to the point: "The doctor said that you are going to die."

The anecdotes say it all, but the lessons may be lost in the intrigue of the stories. Because people and circumstances are different, the lessons in the stories have different faces for different couples. One lesson does not fit all. The Bible allows for that reality. It lays out the ideal with the most potential for benefit. Note that in the third, the doctor suggested a one-way version of the Biblical Model: the wife gives and the husband gets. The Biblical Model works only when both mates agree and faithfully practice.

Toward an effective Marital Dance, this book assumes that both mates are of sound mind and are Christians in name and practice. If these assumptions are not valid, the biblical ideal may be compromised.

The lessons from the anecdotes share a common cause. Before marriage, symbolically, we have only our nest to feather. In marriage, we bring to the table a nest representing who we are and what we have. We can retain control of our nest, share it, or combine it with our mate's nest. What are the implications?

Lesson 1: An Enduring Marriage Starts with Us

After birth, we demand and require attention. The flow is inward, to our needs and wants. In time, we learn effective ways to demand and get more attention. In time, we learn to give to the degree that we get.

The current "you deserve it" culture feeds that mindset. Our nature agrees; we do deserve it. Since life is survival of the fit, we choose to remain fit by getting our share. To ensure our fitness, we will feather our nests for a good today and an even better tomorrow.

When we enter marriage, the *me* mindset and personality come with us. That ego-driven mindset assumes that our spouse is fortunate to have us and is anxious to help feather our (my) nest. Unfortunately, our spouse has the same expectations of us. Obviously, me-centered mindsets sharing the same cocoon are in for a rude shock.

In the tight confines of a marital cocoon, you will see warts (behavioral imperfections) on your spouse that you never saw before. Likewise, your spouse will see warts you never knew you had. Those realities are fertile ground for fighting words to control.

In print, the logic of the above comes through. However, that logic is lost to the power of self-preservation. Before I got married, I was on my own. That reality showed that the greater the effort I exerted, the greater the benefits to me. Looking back, I recall my mother's loving attention to the welfare of her beloved son—me.

Wow, that gave me a heady feeling. The unwritten message was that my mother enjoyed looking after me and wanted to do it. All I had to do was find a mate who enjoyed doting on me as my mother did. Then I could say the traditional "I do" (as in "I do accept your helping hands").

Now for the rest of the story. My wife-to-be, Darlene, stayed at my parents' home for several weeks. After a couple weeks, I asked my mother what she thought of Darlene. Her unexpected answer was out of context with her usual evaluations: "Take her—you won't find better."

Wow! I had never heard my mother speak with such accolades. With that positive endorsement from the best of sources, I asked Darlene if she would help navigate my boat through the waters of life. She agreed.

I read books on what to expect in a mate. My loving wife-to-be fulfilled those expectations and then some. Given my mother's enthusiastic support and the advice from the books, I had it made—or so I thought. I never read about or even considered the other side of the coin: How well did I fit in with and support the needs of my mate?

As you might expect, my me-oriented way of life after several weeks of marriage met its natural end. I came home to a crying wife who noted my lack of attention to her critical needs. Wow! I was unprepared for her response to my being. My only logical response was to change my mindset from "me" to "us." So I did—over time.

The emphasis on "me" dominates most marriages. The reasoning goes like this: "My spouse does not feather my nest, so why should I feather theirs?" Unfortunately, a me-oriented spouse shares the same thoughts. The resulting fights for "feather rights" saps both partners of time, energy, and incentive. The net outcome is a marriage that is destroying your cozy nest. Before long, it becomes apparent that if you are going to have any feathers left, your spouse must go. Consequently, both mates lose.

The above realities lead to lesson 1: to share the same cocoon in a harmonious relationship requires a dramatic shift in mindset from "me" to "us." We need to combine nests to build, share, and enjoy peace and comfort. For the ultimate in stability, durability, and benefits, build your marital nest on a triune foundation defined by Creator God, you, and your mate.

Lesson 2: Certainty Is Based on the Practice of Time-Proven Principles

The above anecdotes dramatically support cause-and-effect behavior that varies with different couples living different lifestyles. The stories indicate that an enduring marriage does not happen by luck but by faithful practice of time-proven behavior by both mates. Behavior starts in the mind, which makes decisions based on emotion and reason. Unrestrained emotions are the reason for undesirable results.

Note that the desired results require that both mates share common strategies to achieve a common goal. To enjoy the benefits, mates must be unified in faith, core values, objectives, and behavior.

We are often encouraged to follow our emotions, to do our thing. However, emotions outside of reason often give us what we don't want. By practicing time-proven behavior, we can go into marriage with the confidence that we can enjoy a lifetime Marital Dance outside the whims of luck. Again, if the mates do not unite toward a common goal, the net result is chance-based—usually destructive to the marriage. To put it another way, it takes two to dance to a familiar tune and choreography.

Hidden in the anecdotes is a critical reality of cause-and-effect behavior: *it is easier to destroy a marital relationship than to build it.* Application of faulty theory or faulty application of proven theory will result in faulty benefits. The benefits can be less than desired in a marital relationship constrained by conflicting realities (as with a couple "unequally yoked"). To ensure an enduring Marital Dance, know and faithfully practice the time-proven BBI and similar time-proven principles.

Lesson 3: To Enjoy an Enduring Marriage, Feather Your Marital Nest

Sharing your nest with your mate is foundational to an enduring Marital Dance. However, it takes more than a shared foundation to make a cozy home that can withstand the storms of life. Mates who are unified in laziness, lack of ambition, and lack of self-control are not going to construct a solid, comfortable nest. The nest they have will atrophy to rubble. Usually, in response to a messy, ill-kept nest, the mates blame each other. However, as the anecdotes show, one of the mates often takes the initiative to clean up and enhance the nest. The lax mate typically comes around to help ensure the comforts of an orderly and well-stocked nest.

The Fourteen Steps, described in Chapter 7, provide the basics for enhancing the marital nest. The practice of basics is foundational to an enduring marital relationship. However, as illustrated in the first anecdote, the marital nest can be stocked with necessities but still be sterile. So what is that magic, missing elixir to joy and happiness in a Marital Dance?

We know that an excellent cake is not baked by chance. It is made by following the instructions in a time-proven recipe. That begs the above question. For an answer, let us go back to the Courtship Dance. In a Courtship Dance, our hormones fuel the desire to be one with another. To win attention, those hormones stimulate a natural outflow, resulting in eros love. Eros love triggers a like response from your potential mate. The cause-and-effect benefits eventually climax in a wedding ceremony.

Eros love is the hormone-driven stimulant that leads to marriage. Agape love is the faith-based music that suggests behavior essential to a joyful, lifetime Marital Dance.

After courtship, the hormonal injections that stimulate eros love atrophy and can go negative. However, the willful practice of agape love can fuel the outflow of eros love. From personal experience and observation, hormonal-driven eros love is for the moment only, like the taste of chocolate. In contrast, combined eros-agape love can fuel the sensory nerves for a lifetime of pleasant memories. Indeed, I can recall the emotions of eros love I experienced during the Courtship Dance with my wife-to-be. Significantly, I also recall the effect of my wife's free-will practice of agape love for my benefit when I was unlovely, with nothing to give except a broken body or spirit.

To help maintain a high level of eros-agape love, consider: next to God, your mate is number one relative to your needs and well-being. Likewise, you are number one relative to the needs and well-being of your mate. Therefore, care for, cherish, nourish, and protect that treasured relationship. The most precious and memorable gift that you can give to your mate is yourself.

Our most memorable marital treasures are independent of wealth. Those treasures are spontaneously born to satisfy the wants and needs of the moment. For example, when I was down, helpless, and unattractive, my wife did what had to be done, including farm chores that were not her thing. That show of love and devotion was more endearing than a physical present. Likewise, when she was down physically or emotionally, agape love showed me how to respond to meet her needs.

We were one in our daily activities. As one, we worked and played. We canoed the wilds, ran a farm, took boat cruises, canned fruits and vegetables, prepared a garden, took bike trips, snow skied, backpacked, rode motorcycles, laughed, cried, and made lovely children—together. As the saying goes, it cannot get any better than that. Indeed, we found that in the Marital Dance, eros love follows because of and due to the effective application of agape love. It is counterintuitive: to receive abundantly from your mate, you must give extravagantly to your mate. In effect, agape love is the nourishment for eros love.

Marital books, the Bible, friends, and relatives suggest ways to make and spread icing onto the wedding cake. The following are fourteen of my favorite recipes that you can modify to ensure that the flames of eros love and the staying power of agape love forever enrich your Marital Dance.

Fourteen Ways to Nourish Eros-Romantic Love

Practice, enhance, perfect, and apply agape love to your mate.

1. Agape love is spontaneous and is shown when least expected: dinner, love notes, etc.
2. Agape love is sacrificial. Massage your mate's weary body with love and tenderness.
3. Spend memorable time together: cycling, skiing, hiking, whatever suits you both.
4. Do the unexpected. Enjoy an early morning breakfast in some quiet, quaint cafe.
5. Plan an annual retreat—just you and your mate.
6. Splurge. The most valuable gift you can give is yourself.

Share your intimate thoughts; know each other; talk and communicate.

7. Express your love and appreciation in writing, song, and touch.
8. Let your mate know by word and deed that they are special.
9. Keep your slate clean. Freely ask for and give forgiveness as needed.
10. Take quiet walks together: hand in hand, to make the unity physical.

Cycle Buddies: Eros-Romantic Love at Its Finest
(The author at 83 and his wife at 81)

Practice eros love in all its wondrous forms and traditions.

11. Revere and hold high birthdays, holidays, and anniversaries.
12. Start a new tradition (e.g., an annual retreat—on Groundhog's Day).

Enhance the romance in your Marital Dance.

13. Do the usual (flowers and gifts) and unusual (a spontaneous weekend trip).
14. Be creative. Show your passion in many wondrous and beautiful ways.

The Biblical Behavioral Instructions (BBI)

Biblical wisdom misapplied is illustrated in the photo and the related text below. Indeed, misapplied biblical instructions can result in discord and needless pain. In the following, note how easily the biblical message can be distorted to support the misleading message of the photo. The photo, as a half-truth, is misleading. The whole truth: I was pushing the wagon, and my wife was guiding and pulling. Together, we did what we could not do individually—the objective of Unity in marriage.

...her household is not afraid of the snow for she bringeth wood from afar...

paraphrased: Prov 31

Biblically Based and Sound (?)

Who can find a virtuous woman? For her price is far above rubies.
Her household is not afraid of the snow, for she is like the merchants' ships;
She bringeth [wood] from afar.
She girdeth her loins with strength and strengthened her arms.
Her husband is known in the gates where he sitteth among the elders of the land.
The heart of her husband doth safely trust in her, for he has no need of spoil.
Her children arise up, and call her blessed; her husband also, and he praiseth her.

— Adapted from Proverbs 31

I rearranged and reworded these verses to match the photo. The original version describes a woman liberated to the full potential of her talents and abilities. The paraphrased version misleadingly describes a virtuous woman as the burden bearer for family needs.

The lesson stands out: Read and study the whole BBI for context and meaning.

Then *be true*, *be sure*, and *practice accordingly.*

Toward an enjoyable, durable Marital Dance, we can develop behavioral guidelines to suit our bent. We can even support our positions biblically by choosing and picking, as illustrated above. However, it is foolish to waste our lives on unproven practices that appear enticing but may have hidden snares. In this book, we will stay with the time-tested BBI.

The Bible can be viewed as a revelation of God or just another book about the Jews and Christians. On theological issues, we cannot comprehend the infinite and know for sure. However, in terms of time-proven behavioral instructions for all areas of life, the Bible has no peer. The biblical guidelines are expressed to the limits of language. Even in the gray areas, behavior is covered by the two Great Commandments of love for God and neighbor (mate). Toward improving and enjoying the Marital Dance, the BBI (mainly from the New Testament) detail the time-tested behaviors to make it happen.

To appreciate the force and power of the BBI, outline the New Testament and pull out all verses that have to do with marital relations and personal behavior. Then let those verses become an integral part of you through ongoing practice.

Relative to effective life management (in behavior, time, money, mind, conflict resolution, decision-making, and more), the Bible encourages us to *be perfect* (complete and balanced) in all areas of life. The challenge is to be an authentic and appealing model of His ways, including the following areas (detailed in the BBI of Appendix I).

- Goals and Objectives
- Commitment
- Performance
- Faith and Works
- Deeds, Work, and Do
- Self-Control
- Personal Development
- Do and Don't Behaviors

- Appearance and Modesty
- Priorities
- False Influences
- Financial Discipline
- Fidelity
- Social/Community
- Family Responsibilities
- Leadership

Authority of the BBI

For most of my Christian life, the New Testament behavioral instructions appeared arbitrary and capricious. Since God said it, don't ask questions; just do it or suffer eternal punishment. That mindset kept me out of mischief, but there was little joy. My objective was legal behavior—to squeak through the pearly gates with the doors closing behind me. As a biblical Pharisee, I was controlled, confined, and constrained by the law. Toward enjoying life by choice, I decided to develop a set of behavioral standards—borrowing, modifying, and creating from whatever source was applicable. So I outlined the New Testament several times and pulled out everything about behavior. I then tested the resultant BBI against quality precepts. The unexpected results turned my thinking inside out.

> **No known treatise on behavior exists that is as complete, thorough, and time-tested as the BBI.**

From the perspective of faith, the BBI are divinely inspired. From the perspective of life, the BBI have been time-tested over the last two thousand-plus years. As such, the BBI represent truth with impeccable certification. No behavioral standard comes with more solid credentials. Having the BBI is like having the winning numbers in the lottery. With the numbers in hand, you cannot lose. Likewise, if the BBI are correctly applied and practiced, you cannot lose. On the other hand, you will lose if you do not practice or your practice is faulty.

After evaluating the results, I had my behavioral standard. I accepted the BBI as is, without reservation or compromise. To enjoy life (marriage) to the max, I now want to know and practice the BBI to the max. In so doing, I will be able to face the adverse events of life with the satisfaction of being mentally, physically, and spiritually fit and prepared. The objective is to be like a marathon runner at the end of a grueling race: exhausted but exhilarated by what was accomplished. As a bonus, you and your mate will benefit from the results of your combined behaviors.

Following is an anecdote that illustrates the benefits of fitness. A doctor hired a highly recommended man to care for his farm. Shortly after he hired the man, there was a terrible storm. Concerned about his farm, the doctor called his new help to see how he weathered the storm. The doctor was shocked to learn that his hired help had slept through the storm. The doctor was furious and told his employee to start packing. On the way to his farm, the doctor noted neighboring farms were littered with dead animals, debris, and the like. He was ready for the worst on his farm, left unprotected by his sleeping help. As he was driving down the lane of his farm, he noted extensive wind damage, broken limbs, and downed trees. Those realities fueled his worst fears.

What he saw at his farm took the wind out of him. He couldn't believe what his eyes told him. His farm seemed to have escaped the brunt of the storm. His livestock were peacefully grazing. The buildings were intact. His sleep-in help was clearing boarded-up windows. "What gives?" the doctor demanded.

The explanation was simple. The hired help heard predictions about the storm and prepared for it. After securing the animals and boarding up the buildings, he was prepared and slept peacefully,

After seeing the total picture, the doctor had to wipe the egg from his face.

To summarize, biblical happiness is a feeling of well-being, contentment, and security consequential to the practice of time-tested behavior. Toward an enjoyable Marital Dance, the verse below, from John 13:17, summarizes the lesson of this section: to be happy, know and do.

IF YOU KNOW THESE THINGS,
BLESSED (HAPPY) ARE YOU
IF YOU DO THEM.

Chapter 4
Twelve Cs for Marital Conduct

During the Courtship Dance, your partner captivated you with their easy flow on the dance floor, their captivating smile, and their charming personality. Wow! You could have danced all night and still have begged for more.

In the Marital Dance, you will dance all day and all night with someone who seems to fill the voids of your life. Then the unthinkable will happen: after many all-nighters, the Marital Dance takes on an unexpected twist. The *wow* of the past becomes an *ow* of the present. The mate who was the rose in your life becomes a thorn in your flesh that grows more irritating with time.

What happened? Why? What can you do for relief?

To answer those questions, let's go back and review the basics. An enjoyable Courtship or Marital Dan*ce* depends on how well the dancers perform to the music and choreography of the dance. In the Courtship Dance, your dance partner is for the moment only. For any reason, you can select a new partner or choose not to dance at all. In contrast, the Marital Dance partner is forever; there is no relief, no reprieve. If your dance partner is an angel, you just died and went to paradise. For you, it can't get any better. If your dance partner is a human being with warts (defects) as big or bigger than yours, you have problems, as does your mate.

There is another critical difference. In the Courtship Dance, the relationship is at a distance, without dependencies. In contrast, the Marital Dance involves an intimate relationship in the confines of a cocoon. In time, each mate will be exposed to their spouse's real and phantom faults. In time, the faults will dominate. The problem is magnified because it is easier to see faults in your mate than in yourself. As such, it can become a contest of fault-finding characterized by stinging verbiage. The evil is that what was said cannot be erased. The echo of the words leaves a scar that is forever, making difficult the restoration of trust.

Warts are a reality. In their worst form, they can be cancerous and destroy the body. Now for the Good News: Our faith can treat and remove warts. For starters, it takes less effort to avoid than to treat them. To prevent warts, fitness is essential. When warts show, the fit Marital Dancer takes immediate steps to remove the wart (remedy the fault).

The fitness of a marital dancer depends on twelve critical, C-defined behaviors: Christian, Compatibility, Commitment, Communications, Conflict (resolution and avoidance), Concentration, Cohabitation, self-Control, Conformance, Consistency, Compassion, and Contentment. Note that some of the Cs are to be embraced and some avoided.

In courtship, look for a mate with the Cs under control. If married, improve your Cs toward a lasting, more enjoyable Marital Dance.

Now let us review, apply, and enjoy.

1. Christian

In a marital relationship, happiness and well-being depend on the character, integrity, and fitness of the mates. *Christianity* is the unifying force that defines these key areaas for mutual practice and benefits. We have only to know, practice, and enjoy.

To ensure a joyful Marital Dance,

I choose to be a Fit Christian Mate who—

- is mentally, physically, and spiritually prepared;
- projects an outward appearance that reflects the inner being;
- is characterized by integrity, decency, and propriety;
- is instinctive with social graces;
- masters time, money, and mind management;
- controls emotions within BBI limits;
- is teachable, accepts criticism, and learns from mistakes;
- strives toward perfection and completeness;
- practices an ongoing fitness improvement program; and
- dances intuitively to the music of agape love and to the choreography and behavior of the BBI.★

★This is the vital quality to ensure a lasting, enjoyable Marital Dance. Test your understanding and practice against the attributes of agape love as detailed in 1 Corinthians 13. Test your dancing skills and marital behavior against the test at the beginning of this book and the BBI summarized in Appendix I.

2. Compatibility

Compatibility is the ability to live in harmony for mutual benefits. For example, the butterfly and flower are mutually dependent (as illustrated in the photo). To benefit, they must live in harmony with each other. Those realities of mutual dependence lead to a primary objective of the Courtship Dance: to find the mate whose needs, merits, and capabilities mesh with and are compatible with your needs and attributes.

There is a caveat: a good partner, who gracefully and charmingly dances the Courtship Dance with you, will not necessarily transfer that grace and charm to the Marital Dance. In contrast, a poor courtship dancer, who is somewhat awkward and clumsy, may be the better mate for the lifetime Marital Dance.

In the Courtship Dance, the exterior catches the eye. In the Marital Dance, the interior defines the person. In the Marital Dance, you and your mate intimately share the same cocoon. In that intimacy, your faults will become focal points similar to a wart on a beautiful maiden. To ensure the

**Compatibility for
Mutual Benefits**

desired benefits, compatibility becomes key. The objective is to be compatible in areas of mutual importance, the basics being faith, character, and core values.

It is not easy to determine who the person is behind a charming persona. For example, a relative of mine was dating a person who seemed to be caring and thoughtful. There were some early countersigns, but the relative dismissed those as anomalies. In time, the relative and the "anomaly" were wed. After becoming one with the family, the new family member showed bipolar attributes of kindness and unkindness bordering on extreme malice and intolerance. Unfortunately, his charm overshadowed the early warning signals. In such a case, wisdom says to hold off until you are reasonably sure you are compatible. To be sure, test against the BBI and confirm with friends and relatives who have your interests at heart but are not emotionally affected by the person.

If confronted by a choice similar to the above, the general guideline is not to marry someone whose character you expect to change after marriage. Most likely, what you see during courtship is only the tip of the iceberg. The iceberg, in most cases, will show its true character during the Marital Dance, when it is generally too late to effect a meaningful change.

In some cases, you may do everything to the Book, and it still will go sour. In search of a mate, my father relied on the judgment of his parents, who saw my mother at her best. Once my father and mother married, her tiger stripes showed, and there wasn't anything my father could do about it. The tiger stripes gave my mother the grit to endure extremely harsh times. Unfortunately for my father, those tiger stripes defined my mother; she backed off from no one. (I saw my mother shake her fist at God for not doing what she thought was His duty.) For such cases, there is no easy answer. To their credit, my parents remained faithful to their marital vows but in isolation from each other. They coexisted, but not as one; they both lost.

Compatibility starts in the Courtship Dance. Choose a mate who reflects your bent in the critical areas of faith, character, integrity, and core values. Next, take compatibility tests to highlight potential areas of conflict. Test against the BBI; confirm with friends and relatives. Give yourself time and space to sort it out.

3. Commitment

The essence of a lasting Marital Dance is born in the will—the *commitment* to hold the marriage vow sacred, come what may.

Before my wife and I were married, we agreed that marriage was a lifetime commitment with no grounds for termination. We honored that commitment such that the word *divorce* never was used in a marital conflict. We knew that to maintain the benefits of Unity, we had to work it out. Sometimes we had long periods of silence to think through the issue. In the end, we knew it was in our interest to make the necessary compromises for a cordial relationship. With age, we learned to concentrate on the 90 percent good and ignore the 10 percent faults, which were generally exaggerated by our emotions.

The following example was told by a minister, whom I will call Bill, about his brother, Joe. The anecdote summarizes the merits and importance of commitment and the will to make it happen.

Joe's parents selected his wife-to-be. Pastor Bill asked his brother a haunting question: "What if you don't like the person our parents selected to be your bride for life?"

In answer to that question, Pastor Bill got a mini sermon from Joe on the essence of a lifetime marital commitment. The crucial factors related to the character and integrity of his future mate. To that end, he trusted his parents to have his best interests at heart. Joe and his betrothed committed to a lifetime relationship with no grounds for separation. Joe looked forward to his upcoming wedding in anticipation of receiving a precious gift with lifetime benefits.

There is no more to be said.

If your potential mate does not share your commitment to marriage for life, it is best to look for another mate. However, if you and your mate embrace a lifetime commitment and dance in unison to the biblical music and choreography, you will have planted the seeds for a sound, lifetime marriage.

4. Communications

Effective *communication* is essential in any relationship, especially in a marital relationship in which you are one with another person. Effective communication comes into play for uniting two minds as one relative to planning, conflict resolution, setting goals and objectives, and so on. Unfortunately, emotions can override reason, making effective communication difficult.

To illustrate the difficulty: at school, English grammar and writing were relatively easy for me. As such, I was hesitant to take a course called "The Dynamics of Effective Communications." On the first day in class, the instructor put my communication skills to the test. The test involved a family of problems and how best to resolve them through *effective* communication. After the test, I was sure I had correctly answered all the questions. Unfortunately, my test score set me back with my tail stuck far between my legs: I got a big, fat, juicy zero, as in all wrong.

Many in the class experienced the same shock. The instructor noted that the test was not a matter of giving the correct answer but identifying the best response for effecting change. He noted that the correct answer can often cause more mischief than no communication. As an example, because of faulty communication, I witnessed discussions in which the end was worse than the start. In one TV episode, an engaged couple disagreed on the vocation of the future wife. The communication on both sides was based on truth, but with emotions overriding reason. At the end of what was intended to be a healing discussion, the engagement terminated in bitterness.

Toward achieving effective communication, apply the Five-Step Plan.

Five Steps toward Effective Communication and Conflict Resolution

The objective of communication in a marital relationship is to unite the couple's strengths into a cohesive force and to help dissolve differences. In good communication, both sides should win;there should be no loser.

Many types of problems involve people with unique peculiarities, strengths, weaknesses, mental maturity, and spiritual maturity. Due to these unique combinations, this section will provide broad guidelines that each couple should tailor to their bent.

It is often necessary that one or both mates change to maintain peace and tranquility. For example, consider a common but complex problem: your mate is obese, adversely affecting their health and your relationship. How can you effectively communicate to achieve change?

Obesity tends to be an emotional issue that is not easily discussed, let alone changed. The obese person knows their condition harms their health and their marital relationship. They also know that they are overweight due to physical reasons or because they overeat and underexercise. The challenge is to communicate toward effective change—in one or both mates as needed.

To effect change, don't tell. Instead, attempt to channel your communication to help your mate recognize their problem and take appropriate steps toward correction. In practice, this is more easily said than done. What if you are the obese mate, or you are both obese? Modify the following procedures as needed to include all permutations of the problem.

1. **Apply agape love with grace.**

   You can't help someone unless you know them relative to their problem.

   How critical is weight loss to your mate? What have they tried?

   What is *their* reason for being overweight?

   Know and empathize with your mate.

2. **Define, understand, and limit discussion to the issue.**

   You cannot resolve a problem you do not understand or that is not clearly defined.

   Is the overweight problem due to overeating or other causes?

   Do you have a common understanding of the problem and its ramifications?

3. **Apply *Enforcers* to ensure the results.**

   Enforcers are any means to help ensure (force) the desired results.

   (e.g., accountability to each other, rewards and penalties, and so on)

4. **List the potential solutions** (with the advantages and disadvantages of each).

   Mental and physical disorders can make an apparent solution unworkable.

5. **Channel the discussion; be prepared to compromise to achieve a realistic plan.**

   Your mate is more likely to accept and follow their plan than yours.

   A clear, detailed plan will cover what, why, and how.

   Guide your mate toward a plan of action (to lose weight),

   The plan should include periodic checkpoints and adjustments to ensure results.

In all failed communications I have witnessed, agape love was missing, resulting in emotional outbursts and personal attacks rather than addressing the issue. Significantly, if emotions gain control, faith and credibility are lost. If that happens, stop! Take a break to allow cooling time.

The Five-Step Plan is simple in concept but difficult in application. The difficulties include:

* motivating you and your mate toward change;
* keeping personal bias out of the process;
* having the time and patience needed to effect change;
* magnifying the problem with potential harm to the marital relationship; and
* losing will and desire to change.

In some cases, it may be best to accept and live with your mate's flaw(s), as they will have to learn to live with your flaws and irritating peculiarities.

5. Conflict Resolution

Since people are different, conflicts are inevitable. Consequently, no method of *conflict resolution* fits all. Unfortunately, an emotionally driven solution to an emotionally driven conflict can spell double trouble. Applying agape love is the first step toward conflict resolution. Counseling may be needed in complex cases (as in financial matters). For most issues, apply the above Five-Step Plan.

To avoid escalating the conflict, agree to limit communication to the issue. Avoid making the issue

Communion or Conflict (?)

personal. If the issue becomes personal, the resolution can become a verbal battle to show that the fault is with your mate. When that happens, call a recess to give both parties time for reason to replace emotion.

For issues that can escalate and get out of control, focus on the cause of the conflict. The objective is for each mate to know and understand the problem and the desired solution through the eyes of their mate. If the resolution process breaks down, delay, allowing emotions to settle. During the pause, pray for wisdom and the courage to practice it.

Consider the lesson from the photo above that shows a symbol of peace (the church) marred by an almost imperceptible instrument of war (a cannon). They are incompatible and contradictory: *return good for evil* versus *get them before they get you*.

The best way to resolve a problem is to take measures to avoid the problem— take the cause of the problem (the cannon) out of the picture. Relative to conflict avoidance, the message is clear: find a mate during your Courtship Dance who augments and supports your faith, ideals, worldview, and way of life. Keep the cannon out of the picture. After marriage, take measures to anticipate and avoid potential problem areas, such as financial planning. For example, my wife and I never had to resolve a financial conflict because we had special planning sessions to minimize that potential (see Chapter 5).

In general, if you and your mate intuitively practice agape love, the frequency and magnitude of conflicts will be minimized. If a conflict shows, *nip it in the bud before it becomes significant.* Consider: you can pull a sapling out by the roots. However, a bulldozer can't budge a mighty oak. Wisdom says to plan accordingly.

6. Concentration

Concentration includes such virtues as attention to detail, awareness, alertness, and the ability to focus mentally, physically, and spiritually on a common need, problem, or issue. In a marital relationship, the above advantages of concentration result in efficiency. An efficiently run household is like a happy sewing machine: effort results in benefits rather than in the costs of fault identification and correction.

To enjoy the desired benefits, plan and *concentrate* accordingly.

7. Cohabitation

In a word, *don't.* There are better, time-proven ways.

Cohabitation can be enticing, innocent in appearance, and appealing to natural desires. Indeed, between consenting adults, one may ask, "Where is the harm? The only difference between marriage and cohabitation is a sheet of paper. That is an insignificant difference. What can go wrong?"

These are fair questions. Let's investigate.

A major motivation for cohabitation is sexual. However, the primary argument for cohabitation is convenience. By living together, a person might argue, "We can save money and get a better feeling for our compatibility toward a stable marital relationship. If it doesn't work, we split without the emotional, legal, and financial pains of divorce." Such reasoning results in the Cohabitation Dance, which prematurely merges the Courtship Dance with the Marital Dance.

The arguments for the Cohabitation Dance are doomed up front. The arguments are ad hoc and without commitment, rules, guidelines, or restraints. The claimed freedom and advantages have hidden nuances that foil the logic. For starters, the couple is constrained only by the emotional eros love that shows its virtues when all goes right. Unfortunately, in life, all does not go according to plan. The stats show that living together out of wedlock will generally reduce, not increase, the chance for a successful marital relationship. There are several reasons for this. First, cohabitation is emotionally driven without constraining guidelines. Second, cohabitation has no built-in response to the critical *what-ifs* that surface in all relationships. Finally, cohabitation assumes life as seen through rose-colored glasses; life is not like that. Significantly, the cohabitation process has all the emotional ramifications of an intimate, marital relationship—without the glue of *commitment*.

Consider the following seven ramifications before you decide to start or continue cohabitation in any of its forms:

1. Behavior has consequences that often affect others. For example, some say that there is no difference between sex inside or outside of wedlock. Tell that to the (estimated) 40 percent of children born out of wedlock (Child Trends, 2016). Most of those children will never know the security of having a father *and* mother. Unplanned parenthood can also result in abortion. Those realities alone should doom cohabitation as a valid lifestyle.

2. Often, the cohabitants have winsome ways. Living together outside of wedlock can appear attractive, innocent, and exciting. However, given that the effects of cohabitation on society are generally harmful, the chain effect of those actions increases the chances for broken relationships, abortion, abuse, and unwanted children. We each have one little life; we should be a positive influence.

3. Before the social revolution of the 1950s, living together out of wedlock was called "shacking up." It was viewed as being similar to prostitution. In both cases, a person gives their body for convenience or money. So why is that lifestyle, so reprehensible yesterday, OK today?

4. By living together before marriage, the couple places little to no value on the most treasured gift they can give: the intimacy of their body to their one-and-only mate for life. Once broken, the fractured ice of fidelity is easily broken again. Broken fidelity ice makes for a fragile marital relationship.

5. Most couples will have children. If sexual relations and living together outside of wedlock are OK for you, then on what moral authority will you guide your children when they choose to live together?

6. Cohabitation is outside the time-proven traditions of marriage held sacred by major religions. On what authority or basis can cohabitation override eons of time–tested tradition?

7. A father wants to make sure that his potential son-in-law is committed and has the strength of character to honor, cherish, and protect his precious daughter throughout life. Likewise, a mother wants her son to enjoy the companionship of a dedicated, devoted wife.

In summary, don't jeopardize your future relationships by taking the cohabitation shortcut to marriage. Why gamble with priceless relationships and future benefits when a viable, time-proven alternative exists in the biblical Courtship Dance?

8. (Self) Control

Self-control is restraint exercised over our impulses, emotions, or desires (Merriam-Webster). Self-control is one of the nine virtues of the Fruit of the Spirit. Self-control is critical to the success of a marital relationship.

What does it mean to exercise self-control? That question is difficult to answer outside of results. As is often the case, the value of self-control is appreciated most when it is lost. When lost, self-control takes on many destructive faces: laziness, physical abuse, gambling, drunkenness, sexual misconduct, smoking, overindulgence, and anything excessive. Lack of self-control, in all its variations, is a root cause for many divorces, based on my personal observations.

Out-of-control problems are due to various reasons: habit, addiction, heredity, freedom to choose, and so on. Unfortunately, not much can be done for the out-of-control person until that person recognizes their problem. That is discouraging. Not only do you have to suffer an unpleasant personality, but you also have to share the consequences of their misconduct with little potential to effect change.

The best way to deal with self-control problems is in the Courtship Dance, during which you can choose not to continue involvement with someone who shows out-of-control symptoms. However, if you are married, the first step relates to spiritual restoration. Sometimes tough love is your only recourse: to stand by and let your mate hit bottom. In many cases, professional counseling will be necessary for you and your mate.

By its nature, self-control is personal. I am responsible for exercising self-control to benefit my mate, family, friends, and self. However, there is a severe problem called *temptation*. Temptation can override reason with emotions of greed, anger, lust, ego, and the like. The Bible has two answers, which I believe are interdependent.

God will not suffer you to be tempted above that you are able. (1 Cor 10:13 KJV)

If your eye offends you, pluck it out, and throw it from you. (Mat 18:9 KJV)

I don't believe there is an answer for the first verse without the second. The second verse appears to be a draconian response to temptation. The eye is essential; it is a magnificent gift. Now we are told to pluck it out. What gives?

A symbolic fence separates us from harmful behavior. If I look over that fence, I will see and desire that which can harm me or my marital relationship. The verse suggests you should give the fence distance by whatever means necessary so that you cannot look over, see, and desire. That is the only way I know how to handle some of my emotionally driven desires.

I have a hypothyroid condition, such that I gain weight easily. My emotions ignore reality and tell me that a doughnut does little harm—eat and enjoy. My mind kicks in and agrees: just one doughnut—eat and enjoy. However, that same mind reminds me that a wee little doughnut a day adds up to 365 doughnuts in a year, enough to give me a doughnut belly and make me an old man before my day. Based on that reality, I know I have to reduce my food intake to low-calorie, nutritious ingredients. I take the doughnuts out of my mind's eye. I am not adversely affected by what I cannot see or do not have. The plan works: I still have hypothyroidism, but I weigh less than I did in my prime in high school.

Many workers in my father's profession were addicted to alcoholic beverages and experienced the associated consequences. Biblically and socially, it is not wrong to drink in moderation. However, in being true to myself, I don't buy the stuff for fear that I could become addicted and lose my self-control, a valuable asset.

The primary reason for a marital relationship is the procreation of new life. That reality results in the most controversial and challenging area of behavior in a marital relationship: sex. To ensure life, the sexual act has pleasurable overtones that can be addictive and override reason. That addiction has a wide range of effects, from the ideal between husband and wife to the evilest encounters imaginable. Between these extremes is the thinking that with present safeguards, sex outside of marriage is acceptable. According to the book *Unchristian* by D. Kinnaman, many Christians (more than 25 percent) believe that sex outside marriage is acceptable—not morally wrong. In the positive, that statistic also means that about 75 percent of Christians believe that sex outside marriage is unacceptable. What is the truth?

I posed that question to myself while in college. My answer: I could not find anyone who could act as an exemplar of safe sex outside of marriage (that is, sex without adverse consequences). If a man after

God's own heart (David) couldn't do it, if the president of the United States (Bill Clinton) couldn't do it, and if the wisest of all men (Solomon) couldn't do it, then what reasonable answer could make me believe that I could do it?

I made a vow to remain faithful to my wife. The only way I know how to keep that vow is to keep my mind pure within marital bounds. Per biblical advice, that means giving temptation distance and avoiding contact. As such, beaches during the high season are out, as are most TV programs and movies.

I know myself. My emotions can easily overwhelm reason. Generally, I have no problem with what I don't see, don't hear, or don't have. The lesson for me is to keep the fence (that separates right from wrong) out of sight and out of mind. A Christian friend once said I wouldn't have to worry about what I saw if I were "filled with the Holy Spirit." That sounds basic, but the many sexual failures by Christian leaders support the biblical wisdom *to flee from* and *pluck it out* if necessary.

The above represent some of my areas for restraint. You may have reasons for restraint in areas in which I am strong. Generally, we do not have to limit our behavior dictated by the weakness of others. However, we need to be honest, authentic, and genuine about our strengths and weaknesses. Biblically, we should restrict our behavior around those who are weak in areas where we are strong.

Take home: to enhance self-control, *be true! If not sure, don't!*

9. Conformance

Conformance is behavior to a specified standard or authority (Merriam-Webster). The standard for the Christian Marital Dance is contained in the BBI. If you and your mate conform to the BBI, you will dance to the same time-proven music, choreography, and behavioral guidelines. As such, compatibility and related benefits are yours to enjoy. Your marriage is secured to the highest level possible (outside the tentacles of mental, physical, and spiritual disorders). Similarly, a flawed understanding or practice of the BBI will result in less than the desired results. Therefore, to ensure a secure, lifetime Marital Dance, conform to and practice an ongoing improvement program as dictated by the BBI.

10. Consistency

Consistency is an innocently appearing word with critical implications for an enjoyable Marital Dance. The words *steady, reliable, uniform, transparent,* and *stable* describe consistency. The definition of each of these adjectives, paraphrased from Merriam-Webster, adds depth and meaning to the word *consistency,* applicable to an enduring marital relationship.

Steady: Stable; not easily upset; constant in principle and purpose; not given to dissipation.

Reliable: Dependable (low failure rate); begins tasks promptly and finishes work begun.

Uniform: Consistent in appearance, word, and conduct.

Transparent: Free from pretense or deceit; readily understood.

Stable: Steadfast, steady, staunch, unwavering, and not emotionally driven.

From the above, consistency is *constant* and therefore predictable. To be constant is to have a character defined and constrained by *integrity*. Integrity, nourished by agape love, is the root of all behavior. In its basic form, *integrity is honesty* that covers a large spectrum. Integrity is uncorrectable, sound, complete, and uncompromising in morals or ethics. As such, integrity is essential to the development of trust. Trust is foundational to an enjoyable and enduring Marital Dance. Indeed, the strength of the marital bond can be determined by the level of trust between the mates. Again, trust has its roots in integrity that is consistent.

Now let us review consistency in application.

Occasionally, I can hit a tennis ball as well as a pro. Despite that reality, I am still far from the winner's circle. The overriding reason is that my good shots are by accident; the pro's shots are *consistent*. You can't predict my shots, but you can predict the pro's shots with near certainty. The difference is consistency. If you want to win consistently at the game of tennis, you must be consistent with your winning shots. Relative to marriage, consistency builds trust, perhaps the most critical virtue in an enduring, happy Marital Dance.

In a marital relationship, consistency has many measures depending upon the nature of the behavior. For example, 99 percent trustworthiness would generally be considered a good standard of consistency. However, to be 99 percent faithful to your mate would be overshadowed by a 1 percent failure rate. That reality is called *adultery*. Indeed, that 1 percent failure rate can be sufficient grounds for divorce. Failure in some aspects of life can be tolerated; in others, 100 percent consistent, failure-free performance is required. Adultery can be forgiven, but its scars are forever. As such—*don't!*

The hallmark of quality is consistency. A quality person or mate consistently performs to standard. In general terms, quality is consistently fit for use.

A "Quality Mate" consistently and predictably performs to the BBI.
To ensure an enduring, happy, Marital Dance, be a Quality Mate.

11. Compassion

Compassion is a sympathetic awareness of another's distressed needs together with a strong desire to help alleviate them (Merriam-Webster). Unfortunately, a spouse's needs are often emotionally fed, making healing difficult. As usual, start with an agape-love mindset that is focused on the well-being of your spouse. Indeed, it would be difficult, if not impossible, to practice compassion outside the influence of agape love.

Since we are emotionally driven, it is comforting to have mates who can help us through the riptides of life. To ensure a compassionate spouse for your mate, include compassion in your arsenal of assets.

12. Contentment

Contentment is a condition of the mind that is free from wants or desires. Relative to a happy, enduring marriage, contentment with life and your spouse says it all. Yet, paradoxically, some people seemingly have it all except contentment. Others who have only the essentials show a contented face. So what is contentment?

My niece walked into a horse barn and remarked, "It smells good in here." Her brother immediately countered, "No, it doesn't; it stinks." The same environment with the same smells evoked conflicting responses of contentment and discontentment.

Contentment is born in the mind and trained accordingly. Apostle Paul in Philippians 4:11 says, "I have learned to be content in whatever state I am." To feed contentment, start the day with a spirit of thanksgiving for what you have, and do not dwell on what you do not have.

The Face of Contentment is Unstressed and Satisfied

A stress-free environment is the dance floor of contentment. Therefore, plan and live today toward a stress-free tomorrow. For example, it is difficult to be content while drowning in an ocean of debt. In effect, the BBI contains the seeds that, if properly planted and tended, will provide a bountiful harvest of blessings for a contented tomorrow.

The objective: enact the causes today that will effect a bountiful harvest tomorrow.

Summary

To ensure harmony in the confines of a marital cocoon, the needs and behavior of each mate must mesh with, augment, and support the other. To make it happen, know, practice, and conform to the Twelve Cs.

For incentive, imagine that your behavior in each of the Twelve Cs results in a warm fuzzy if correctly applied and a burr if misapplied. Remember, your cocoon contains the fuzzies and burrs produced by you and your mate. No sane person would ever want to leave a cocoon lined with fuzzies. Similarly, the burrs give a person reason to want out.

For mutual benefit:

      Decorate your marital cocoon with fuzzies.

      Develop abhorrence of the sight and nature of burrs.

Chapter 5
Insurance Measures

With the one little life we each have, we want to take the necessary measures to ensure an enduring, joyful Marital Dance. Hence, we need to be prepared to pay for the insurance. The insurance costs are minuscule compared to the emotional and monetary costs of a broken marital relationship. This chapter will concentrate on the costs and related benefits of five basic insurance measures. To be a quality mate, apply all insurance measures to all areas of life. For maximum enjoyment, the objective is to function at your God-given best, spiritually, mentally, physically, economically, and behaviorally.

This chapter will use math to illustrate and confirm principles and conclusions. Detailed supporting math is provided in Appendix III. In math, the unit of measure can be anything: dollars, talents, burrs, or fuzzies. For illustrative purposes, most appreciate the difference between ten and a hundred dollars. In contrast, what does it mean to have ten or a hundred talents? Accordingly, we will use the dollar as the unit of measure to illustrate a principle.

1. Faith

A happy marital relationship may happen by chance, as in winning the lottery. However, to enjoy consistent benefits, it is necessary to apply time-proven standards such as the BBI. Since anyone can apply and conform to the BBI, what are the benefits of faith?

In response to that question, books are written with pro and con arguments about the benefits of faith. To me, the reasons for faith are overwhelming. Without faith, I probably would respond similarly to an atheist friend with whom I enjoyed playing squash. He believed that there was no God and held to a consequential worldview.

According to his worldview, since there is no Creator, human beings have no more value than a twig, an accident of nature with momentary purpose only. Accordingly, the law of the land is *survival of the fit* with no right and wrong. (A twig does what it does; it can do no wrong, nor can it do right.)

Consequently, he noted that the only reason he was civil was that he enjoyed playing squash with me. To ensure a playing partner, he knew he had to maintain acceptable levels of friendship. He then noted that he would have no qualms of conscience to finish me off if it served his purpose, and there would be no adverse repercussions.

Solid Faith, Solidly Anchored

My friend treated me with respect and was a good sportsman. Given what he said, I thought it best not to test his worldview.

My friend's worldview of survival of the fittest twigs has been held by leaders who ordered some of the greatest atrocities known to man. To those leaders, we were all twigs of insignificant value. For one who holds that faithless worldview, a marital relationship is like a house built upon the sand—without a foundation. It is fragile, for the moment only. Whatever happens in the marriage is accidental, without purpose or value.

The twig reasoning is shallow and without merit or benefit. A twig cannot shape its future. In contrast, humans have the intelligence to build skyscrapers, bridges that cross "impossible" gorges, and planes that can outdistance the speed of sound. Twigs have no such potential. It is the limit of foolishness to be made in the image of a super Creator and then be self-constrained to the realities of a twig. We have fantastic reasoning and creative abilities to ensure a good today and an even better tomorrow. Twigs have no such potential.

Thank God that we are not twig-bound.

As persons of faith, my wife and I are committed to practicing the biblical Constitution of Behavior. A couple without faith has no constitution to dictate their behavior, outside the constraints of law and the mores of friendship. They can choose to accept, modify, or reject whatever suits their whim. Accordingly, they are confined to the limits of chance and their tolerance level. Any bonding is for the moment only and then only for personal benefit. In contrast, by accepting the time-proven BBI, my wife and I build upon inspired wisdom honed to perfection through eons of time. Twigs have no heritage, incentive, or mandate to build upon the knowledge of past twigs.

The skeptic responds, "From what I have observed, I see no difference in the divorce rate of Christians versus non-Christians." My own studies and observations confirm his conclusion. Implicit in his rebuke is the conclusion that there is little to no benefit in applying the constraints of the Christian faith to a marital relationship. Indeed, why practice a philosophy that constrains without benefit?

For certain, that statistic is discouraging and damaging. It should never be. In response, let's look at the primary reason for the high divorce rate among Christians. In my last twenty-plus years of church attendance, I recall no sermons or Sunday school lessons on the sanctity and holiness of a marital relationship or how to keep it holy. You cannot win a ball game if you don't know the rules or how to play. Likewise, you cannot experience the results of faith-based behavior if you do not know and faithfully practice the specified behavior.

That reality takes us to the critical question: What is the benefit, if any, of faith to the success of a lifetime Marital Dance? As a starting point, faith has merit only to the extent that it is known and practiced. In the church of my youth, a lifetime marital commitment was a basic tenet of the faith, not open to compromise. Accordingly, I knew of no divorce in our church denomination during the first eighteen years of my life. That reality gives credence to the BBI.

At this point, my skeptic friend would interrupt, "If I desire, I can adopt the Bible as my standard of behavior. I can accept and practice as I wish without believing in an unimaginable divine origin."

True, he can accept or reject whatever he wishes. However, overriding his freedom to accept or reject is his worldview that we have no more value or purpose than a twig. Applied, this means he and his mate are mere twigs without purpose or reason. Consequently, there is no right or wrong behavior. One's acceptance of the Bible is conditional upon its potential benefit to oneself. As my friend noted, at any moment, for any reason, he would have no qualms about using whatever means to satisfy his perceived desires. Now consider that his mate has the same worldview. Under those conditions, unity and its benefits are impossible. Personal benefit overrides the needs and desires of one's mate. That worldview is foundational to conflict—*Get them and theirs before they get you or yours.* Given those realities, I would not want to be the mate of someone who holds me no higher than a twig.

Consider: you and your mate are lost in the wilderness—dependent on each other for survival. Would you prefer a Christian mate who treasures your life as their own, or an atheist who lives by the law of the fit? If my atheist friend and I were lost in the wilderness, I would fear him more than the realities of the wilderness. In a marital relationship, that lack of trust can be deadly, with no compensating potential for benefit.

My atheist skeptic is persistent. He notes that laboratory and field results verify evolutionary theory. Therefore, we need to adjust our thinking to that reality. The Bible may be time-proven, but it has no more merit than any other time-proven work by man.

For some work I was doing, I needed to understand the validity of the foundational arguments for evolution. I expected to spend at most a month. From the start, I saw flaws in the theory that violated system-based principles that are time-proven. I spent more than five years applying my expertise in complex systems development (as found in every life form) to the arguments of evolution. My conclusion: evolution is a fact as claimed in its ability to change the appearance of a species. It is fiction in its claim to have evolved new life forms. My conclusions are based on comprehensive and convincing margins showing that natural forces do not have the mutational work potential or the systems knowledge required to evolve new, novel, interdependent, critical systems that define each unique species.

To fill the void left by the chance-based theory of evolution, a super-intelligent reality has to be. We call that reality *Creator God*. Historical records show that the Creator desires the best for His prized creation—the human species. Accordingly, our Creator laid down the basics toward enjoying a full and abundant marital relationship.

Maybe an atheist can enjoy a lifetime marital relationship without faith—maybe. However, with one little life, I don't want to chance it. I will choose a marital relationship with a person of practiced faith any time over a person who values life on par with a twig.

I am satisfied that faith is foundational toward enjoying a lifetime marital relationship. To ensure the desired results—

Be True: Behave and Practice Accordingly!

2. Excellence

Excellence, according to Merriam-Webster, means "eminently good." It follows that if your Marital Dance is excellent, you and your mate will enjoy the excellent benefits. That is the objective: to strive for excellence to enjoy optimum benefits and avoid harmful consequences.

We know couples who go by the Book, and still they do not enjoy the expected benefits. They work hard and follow biblical principles, but their lives are chaotic, resulting in strained marital relations. My parents are examples of that contradiction. They were religious, hardworking people, yet their marriage contradicted the intensity of their faith. After my father's death, I wept upon reading his well-worn Bible, filled with underlined verses. "Poppa, you read and studied but couldn't apply. Why? What was missing?"

Unfortunately, the above is common to many Christian couples who do not enjoy the promised benefits of their faith. I was given a similar problem at work: "We are applying the basics, doing the best we know, and still our products are performing poorly. Find out why and what should be done."

I started with the fundamentals. What is required to make a sewing machine (or a married couple) sing a happy tune while it faithfully does its thing, day in and day out, come what may? What is the mark of excellence for the daily Marital Dance?

Toward an answer, let's start with the basics. A Marital Dance of excellence requires a quality Christian couple (mature disciples) who effectively use their time to the limits of their talents and resources. With regard to achieving excellence, the emphasis is on the word *effective*.

There is a hidden *gotcha* in the above statement. Consider: you give part of your life, measured in time, to work for money. It follows that if you waste money or resources, you waste or squander part of your life.

If you waste or squander, you gain no benefit from that time. Unfortunately, wasted time can have negative consequences mentally, physically, and spiritually. As such, it is possible to work hard and then foolishly waste the benefits of that life and labor. Lack of benefit is not the hallmark of excellence.

Mindset

The level of excellence achievable starts in the mind—what it believes it can and cannot do. Your mind can be enhanced or degraded by what your mate thinks of you.

My parents serve as negative exemplars of that reality. My father and mother were talented, diligent, self-disciplined, and Christian. Those virtues should have ensured a near-ideal marital relationship—but they didn't. The reason falls primarily on my mother, who stripped my father of any worth by verbiage honed to razor-sharp perfection. In German, she denigrated my father in harsh terms: "An ox has more sense in its horns than you have in your head." In response, my father found little reason to hold my mother in high esteem. They effectively reduced each other's stature and potential. Consequently, they endured where they should have prospered. With a mindset focused on their mate's perceived faults, neither could concentrate and work toward a common good and goal.

In the positive, I am grateful to my mother, who advised, "Take her [referring to my wife-to-be]; you will not find better." So I took her and became one with a jewel, leading to another wonder of life: the better I cherish my wife as a jewel, the more radiant she becomes. The more radiant becomes my jewel, the greater becomes the treasure.

To illustrate the magnifying power of a jewel relationship, consider the lesson from an old anecdote, "The Seven-Cow Wife," which I retell from memory.

On Paradise Island, the primary topic of the discussion groups centered on Bachelor Joe, who had it all: looks, charm, and social status. Significantly, he was also the son of the wealthiest, most prestigious family on the island. The islanders watched Bachelor Joe as a hawk watches its prey. Who was he courting? Where did the couple go? What did they wear? These questions provided the energy that fueled the discussion groups. The big question: Who would Bachelor Joe choose to be the first lady, worthy of the crown as queen of Paradise Island?

As is often the case, reality is stranger than fiction. The discussion groups were faced with an unexpected twist that defied their reasoning. Bachelor Joe was courting a common young woman with a common face, the common name Lucy, and a common heritage from the common side of the island. The discussion groups wondered: Why, what, and how? What attributes did Lucy have above all the other maidens of the island? How did Bachelor Joe meet a young woman from the common side of the island? How would she hold his attention?

Time supplied the answers. Lucy not only held Bachelor Joe's attention, she was the focal point of his attention. That gave fuel to the most tantalizing of all discussions. On that island, it was customary for the groom's family to give the bride's family a gift for the right to change her family name. Typically, the gift was one, two, or at most three cows. There was no public record of there ever being a four-cow exchange. Based on custom, the bargaining power of Joe's family, and Lucy's common heritage, the betting odds were that Lucy's family would receive two cows.

The negotiation started with the traditional dinner. After dinner, all were in relaxed, amenable moods, perfect for achieving the desired three-cow agreement. Joe's father started the discussion by noting the advantages Lucy would gain with her new family name. He made some other statements that suggested a bottom offer of one cow. After a little more talking, Lucy's father asked the big question: "What is your offer?"

Joe's father noted Lucy's extraordinary qualities and how his family had already accepted her. Then he made a remarkable offer of five cows.

Lucy's father choked, and her momma fainted. Lucy's brothers and sisters looked like shocked zombies. Joe's father read these signs as disappointment with, if not rejection of his offer. Fearful of losing Lucy, he apologized for the low offer and raised it to seven cows. The evening ended as a profitable and memorable event for all.

The drama was still in the larval stage; it hadn't morphed into its final glory. Joe and Lucy were married and went off on their honeymoon. In their absence, the discussion groups debated the outcome of a two-cow wife trying to live up to seven-cow expectations. Group wisdom declared that there was no way that a two-cow reality of common heritage could bridge the vast chasm to the seven-cow performance expected in her new, prestigious setting.

The honeymooners returned from their trip, greeted by a large group of friends, well-wishers, and curious onlookers from the discussion groups. As the couple got off the plane, the onlookers were unprepared for what they saw. Joe walked off the plane with a stunning young woman by his side who had the beauty, confidence, and grace of a gazelle. The reaction was immediate and visceral. As expected, the marriage hadn't lasted, but for Lucy's sake, Joe could have given her more time. In that short period, Joe had replaced Lucy with a new, exotic import in keeping with his position and stature on the island. Feelings toward Joe turned negative. How could he have been so cruel to Lucy?

But wait! It can't be! As the couple walked toward the crowd, it hushed in shocked silence. That stunning young woman looked familiar. As the couple walked closer, the image of the mysterious woman came into focus. The attractive woman by Joe's side was Lucy, who now gave witness to her right to hold the crown of a worthy, seven-cow wife. She thereby established a new benchmark of excellence for all the island maidens.

The lesson is fundamental: hold high the virtues of your mate. Still, that alone will not ensure excellence in the marital relationship. Marriage involves *two* united as *one* toward a common goal. Your enjoyment in the Marital Dance will depend upon your excellence: how effectively you work and play together.

Life Viewed through Christ-Tinted Glasses

The foundation of excellence is the words *I can*. If your mind says, "I can do all things through Christ" (Php 4:13), then you can. In contrast, if you think the words *I can't*, you can't!

Relative to "I can," the Bible emphasizes the nobility of work. That emphasis is supported by a clipping I took from a publication by the University of Cincinnati (circa 1960).

> The greatest analgesic, soporific, stimulant, tranquilizer, narcotic, and to some extent even antibiotic—in short, the closest thing to a genuine panacea known to medical science is work.

From a lifetime of observations, I would expand the above. In terms of a happy marital relationship, the closest thing to a genuine panacea is a marital couple effectively working as one toward a common goal.

Failure to work effectively together is cause for disharmony and divorce. Despite our human frailties, my wife and I know that we benefit from the work of each other. We cherish those benefits.

Significantly, the biblical emphasis on work does not end in retirement. Reality says that we will eventually lose our abilities to work and do. It is also reality that *we will lose it sooner if we don't use it*. That reality contains hidden gems. First, work has blessings and benefits toward a better tomorrow. The negative is equally significant: if you don't work, there is no benefit. Tomorrow will be worse than it has to be.

The ability to work, create, and do are precious gifts from God. With the facility to create, we have godlike capabilities. After my triple-bypass heart surgery, I could do no work. I recall praying, "Lord, please hasten the day when I am whole again and can work. Forgive me if I ever complain about the work that You privileged me to do." I have many exemplars who championed the benefits of that prayer. On my way to work, I often saw a pretzel-twisted old man who didn't know the words *can't* or *quit*. As long as there was life, he would work. I often saw him, curled like the letter C, pushing a wheelbarrow at less than a snail's pace. If he can, then with God's help, so can I.

The Author (at 73), **Practicing What He Preaches**

I decided early in life to apply the biblical precept "Through Christ, I can do." After triple-bypass heart surgery, two hip replacements, a knee replacement, and other surgeries, I still *can do*, as shown in the above photo. Now, at age eighty-nine, I can still do rock work, split wood, and the like. It takes longer—sometimes much longer. To keep mentally and physically fit, I exercise (work, ride my bike, whatever) for half the day. The other half is spent in mental exercise—study and writing. The blessings flow consequentially to the behavior. Thank You, Lord!

Most will not pay the price for excellence because the costs appear greater than the perceived benefits. It costs more to get an A grade than a C. At the time of grading, there is no apparent benefit for the extra effort to get the A. The benefit, if any, is delayed into the future. In some cases, the added benefits do not justify the added costs. College degrees, for example, can come with huge debt burdens. Given those realities of excellence, how do you ensure a cost-effective marital relationship?

To ensure positive results, start with step 1 toward excellence: be true to God, yourself, and your mate. Then consider the related mathematics that show a range from extreme consequences to spectacular benefits, depending on the level or lack of excellence in your marital relationship.

To illustrate the long-term benefits of excellence, the following example is based on *talents*, a unit of measurement that relates to your moral fiber, knowledge, capabilities, and wealth—all that defines who you are and what you can do. For ease of understanding, I use dollars for the unit of measure in the equations. Relative to benefit and personal application, replace the word *dollars* with the word *talents.* Consider: a dollar spent is gone. In contrast, a talent withers and dies if not used and exercised.

Two young men, Tom and Bill, graduate from high school with $100 each. Tom is laid back and enjoys life as it comes. He averages a 5 percent loss of his assets each year. At the end of the first year, he still had a comfortable reserve of $95—no cause for concern or lifestyle change.

Bill also enjoys life, but he puts forth a little extra effort. He enjoys a 5 percent growth rate of his assets each year. At the end of the first year, he has $105—not enough to make a difference in his lifestyle. Given the insignificant difference at the end of the first year, Bill wonders if Tom has it right. However, trusting the ageless wisdom of the Bible and his elders, Bill holds to his constant 5 percent growth rate.

At their twentieth class reunion, Tom has only 36 of his original 100 dollaars [$(0.95)^{20}$ x 100 = 35.8]. Tom struggles to keep his head above water; he has nothing to give, and society takes the little he has. Tom is bitter. That bitterness increases when he sees Bill.

Bill enjoys the good life, as witnessed by his poise, dress, and demeanor. Fortunately, Tom doesn't know the whole truth. Twenty years ago, the two men had equal assets of $100 each. Now, Bill has $265 [$(1.05)^{20}$ x 100 = 265], and Tom has only $36 [$(0.95)^{20}$ x 100 = 35.8].

The situation gets worse. At the forty-fifth class reunion, the (mathematical) score is $10 to $900 (at the 5 percent rates) in favor of Bill. With only ten dollars, Tom is bitter with everyone and everything, including his wife and his God. From Tom's perspective, God has His favorites. Tom compares his wife (who has suffered because of Tom's mediocrity) to Bill's wife. If he had a wife like Bill's, he thinks, he would have something to show.

In contrast, Bill's storehouse is bursting at the seams. Bill's wife has benefited from his disciplined lifestyle; because of this, she willingly became one with Bill, thereby enhancing his decision-making. Bill gives and gives more from an overflowing storehouse that seems to be self-filling. Bill praises his God for bountiful blessings and a lovely wife.

(See Appendix III for the detailed math to support the above.)

The math explains why some couples are bitter and seek divorce in their senior years. Others tolerate their mates. A few enjoy their last Marital Dances with the euphoria of their first Courtship Dances. When the lights dim, they are still joyfully dancing as one. That is the objective.

Assume that you had the aggressive personality of Bill but were married to someone with Tom's satisfaction with mediocrity. How long do you think the joy in that marital relationship would last? Worse, assume that you and your mate had Tom's mediocre drive. The compounded negative results would stress the saints to the breaking point. A mediocre person usually blames their mate for their so-called bad luck. Magnify that reality when both mates are mediocre. They may *coexist*, but with little to nothing to show, they certainly will not *coenjoy.*

True, nuanced circumstances can alter the results dramatically. However, if your excellence reflects unblemished fruit of the Spirit (as recorded in Gal 5:22), you will enjoy your marital relationship regardless of the circumstances. That is the objective: come what may, you and your mate are prepared to ride out the rough waters.

Time Management

Let's concentrate on the second step toward excellence: effective time management. This section will cover time management in terms of balance, priority, and finish. But first, we will review Pareto's principle, based on the 80/20 rule, which is fundamental to successful time management. (Pareto's principle is a generalization that says it takes significantly more of your time as you strive toward a higher level of perfection, finish, or grade.)

Pareto's principle says *life is not linear* (a straight line). In a linear relationship, 80 percent of the people do 80 percent of the work. According to Pareto, as a general statement, 20 percent of the people do 80 percent of the work. Similarly, 20 percent control 80 percent of the wealth, 20 percent cause 80 percent of the mischief, and so on. In terms of excellence, perfection at 100 percent represents excellence at its limit. Following Pareto, it will generally take 20 percent of one's work time to complete a task to the 80 percent finish level. It will take the other 80% of one's time to reach the highest level of excellence possible, near-perfection. (Perfection is probably not achievable, definable, or desirable, given the horrendous cost burden for an insignificant incremental gain.)

In a marital relationship, many tasks must be completed in a fixed amount of time. How you do or don't do those tasks will reflect on the excellence of your Marital Dance. Critical, uncompleted tasks fuel marital flare-ups and controversy. In effective time management, decisions and related actions are based on priority, balance, and finish.

Priority, Balance, and Finish

Life consists of decisions to be made and tasks to be completed. Those decisions and tasks can be prioritized into three levels:

A. Critical with time constraints
B. Critical with relaxed time constraints
C. Nice, but not necessary or critical

All the above can be completed with a finish grade of 80 percent, to a fine-furniture level (near perfection). Balance can change the priority and finish of any of the above. Typically, work-related decisions are of A or B priority. However, if work-related projects become dominant, to the neglect of wife or family, balance comes into play. Often, for example, a professional person must be on the road, to the neglect of family. In that case, decisions and tasks must be reprioritized. To maintain a reasonable degree of balance between work and family, a C task may become an A task.

In other cases, an A task can become a C task due to pressure from unforeseen events. For example, an A task of family devotions has C priority when the house is on fire. Similarly, a work-related A task has C priority if your mate is critically ill or has severe issues with you.

There is a problem: to ensure an enjoyable, long-term Marital Dance, the objective is for the mates to become excellent dancers working toward ever-higher levels of excellence. However, according to Pareto's principle, as you approach perfection, the cost in time and resources can become enormous, outweighing hoped-for benefits. Worse, the quest for perfection in one area can result in horrendous costs of mediocrity in other areas.

For example, an associate female employee enjoyed the prestige of fast-track advancements for her exemplary work. It was a heady experience. In response, she gave her all toward perfection at work, sacrificing personal and family needs. The result was that I met her in the hall, and she was crying. The demands of her job were overwhelming, draining her lifeblood. In time, the job separated her from her husband and family. She had prestige and money in her pocket, but she didn't have what mattered.

I saw similar situations repeated in the positive and negative. I know people who gave up managerial positions that would have robbed them of precious family time. A woman who was a lawyer and a friend gave up her high-paying profession for a critical, nonpaying job—at home with her children. If necessary, she could resume her profession, but she couldn't recapture lost time with her family. Many would have chosen the monetary option; however, I believe she correctly assessed balance and priority and acted accordingly.

Desirable products with premium benefits are built to the highest standards. Likewise, to enjoy a premium marital relationship and benefits, strive for excellence in your Marital Dance by moving flawlessly and gracefully to the rhythm of agape love. Those pretty words have little to no meaning outside of application. So let us apply.

The highest standards of conduct are prescribed for those in church leadership, who should be exemplary in all areas of life. Those high standards of conduct and behavior are also foundational to a premium Marital Dance (see 1 Tim 3:2–4, 8–11; Titus 1:6–8, 3:8–11).

Here are the guidelines for maximum marital benefit.

Be an Excellent Dancer who—

- ➢ loves what is good and holy;
- ➢ is respectable and blameless;
- ➢ is not a lover of money or pursuer of dishonest gain;
- ➢ loves and is devoted to your mate;
- ➢ has faithful, obedient children;
- ➢ is self-controlled, temperate, and disciplined;
- ➢ is not given to much wine or drunkenness;
- ➢ is hospitable;
- ➢ is not violent, overbearing, quarrelsome, or quick-tempered;
- ➢ teaches the truths of faith;
- ➢ is tested—of proven character;
- ➢ is not a malicious or slanderous talker;
- ➢ is sound in faith, in love, and in endurance; and
- ➢ is of sound speech that cannot be condemned.

3. Harmony

IN HARMONY

The above photo suggests the advantages of living in harmony with each other and the environment. *To live in harmony* requires that all contribute to a common good. From another perspective, to enjoy the benefits of harmony, we obviously must live in harmony—with our *ducks in a row* and *under control*. So how do two people, who are physically different, live in and enjoy the benefits of a harmonious Marital Dance?

The Bible (as detailed in the BBI) foresaw the question and provided the answer in the simplicity of these words: the fruit of the Spirit. The fruit of the Spirit, as defined in Galatians 5:22, 23, is the nourishment of marital harmony. For ever-ready and intuitive application, memorize Galatians 5:22 and give it center stage in your daily activities.

Note that the verse has an anomaly: it is not *fruits* (plural) of the Spirit but the singular *fruit* of the Spirit. The singular fruit of the Spirit is the Vital One, characterized by nine virtues or nutrients. The nine virtues are inclusive, as in being total and complete. Of significance, the first and most crucial virtue or nutrient is agape love. The other eight virtues relate to the behavior and character of the dancers.

To apply, think through the ramifications of each virtue relative to behavior and its effects—especially when your mate is at their frustrating worst. In that case, review each virtue and then ask the pertinent question: Has this virtue gone sour? If so, what do I (we) need to do to restore its vitality?

To ensure an Enduring and Joyful Marital Dance,
Be Fit, as defined by the Nine Virtues of
The (Golden) Fruit of the Spirit. (after Gal 5:22, 23)

FRUIT of the SPIRIT

*** LOVE ***

Is the parent of all virtues. It is characterized by a loyal, unselfish,
and benevolent concern for the good of your mate.

*** JOY ***

Is an inward, unconditional state of happiness and well-being.

*** PEACE ***

Is freedom from troubling or oppressive thoughts and emotions.
It results in a form of tranquility and quiet harmony.

*** PATIENCE ***

Forbears under provocation. It is steadfast despite opposition or adversity.
Patience is not impulsive; it endures affliction without complaint.

*** KINDNESS ***

Is consequential to agape love. Its face is pleasant, sympathetic, and forbearing.
Kindness is outgoing; it gives pleasure or relief.

*** GOODNESS ***

Is consequential to behavior that conforms to the BBI.
Goodness is virtuous, righteous, commendable, benevolent, and well-behaved.

*** FAITHFULNESS ***

Is being steadfast, loyal, and uncompromising to the welfare of your mate.
Faithfulness is not likely to desert or betray.

*** GENTLENESS ***

Is mildness in manners and disposition; it is free from harshness or violence.

*** SELF-CONTROL ***

Is restraint exercised over one's impulses, emotions, or desires.
(The above are based on biblical context and definitions by Merriam-Webster)

To live in harmony, we must be true to God, to our mate, and to ourselves.

Be True to God

To be true to God, you and your mate must accept and faithfully practice His ways. It is a lifetime quest to know and faithfully practice His ways in all areas of life. There can be no compromise. To win consistently at the marital game, it is *His way all the way.*

His way all the way: to some, that phrase is hard-line and radical. It comes across as meaning *do it without question.* That is not the intention or message. Consider: you enjoy tennis and want to play the game at your best. You know a tennis coach whose record shows that he is the best of the best. You are a good player with a need for improvement, so you sign on. After taking several lessons, you note little to no improvement because you insist on playing the game your way. As such, your progress is limited to the potential of your way. You are not taking advantage of the lessons your coach can teach you.

Signing on with God as your Coach has no merit outside of total acceptance and practice of His ways. If the coach is time-proven, and if you accept and apply that coach's lessons, you will experience improvement. With improvement, you will want to know and apply more of the winning ways of your coach.

As a personal example, I thought I was a good checkers player—until I played a fellow worker. As a good player, I lost at least thirty-five games before winning a single game. After a few games, it was evident that he was a master player, and so he was—a top-seated player in the state. From then on, I was privileged to learn from the best, so I did. I played checkers his way. In time, I could beat him in two of five games. That didn't put me in his league, but it gave me a significant advantage over my peers.

To enjoy a delightful, enduring marital relationship, *dance His way all the way.*

Be True to Your Mate

Being true to your mate is the first step toward being of *one flesh* with your mate. Symbolically, you became one flesh with your mate when you agreed to become a lifetime partner with your mate. Note that half of that agreement is on your side. If you are true to each other, the desired results are the consequence. To enjoy the results of Unity, be one with your mate—in all areas of life.

In a marital relationship, husband and wife share the same cocoon. In the confines of that cocoon, each will become intimately familiar with the other's strengths and weaknesses—physical, mental, and spiritual. Each mate will bear the burden of both their and their mate's misbehavior. Similarly, they will also share the benefits of their combined constructive behavior. It follows that time-proven behavior on the part of both mates is foundational to an enjoyable lifetime relationship.

The above consequences are easily lost in today's individualistic society, in which the motto seems to be "No one is going to tell me what to do or how to live." Those words are empty and without merit.

When sharing a cocoon, you can still do your thing. In the extreme, you are free to feed your ego with the excitement of an extramarital affair. However, you are not free to escape the built-in consequences. For all misbehavior, payday comes in the form of burdensome debt, disease, unwanted children, loss of a loving marital relationship, and, in extreme cases, death.

The above realities are compounded by the intimacy of a marital relationship within the confines of a cocoon. Your mate exercised their freedom, and now you must pay for some or all the consequential costs. As witnessed by the high divorce rate, most people do not want to pay for the misdeeds of their mate.

To appreciate the above toward intuitive application, review the BBI as summarized in Appendix I. Test each guideline against the results. Is this behavior going to add or detract from our marital relationship? Make it personal: Do I want my mate to be characterized by this behavior? With one little life, with one critical Marital Dance, you want to be sure. To gain that certainty and make it happen to the limits of your potential, practice and apply the BBI.

Take home: being true to your mate starts with being true to the ways of your Maker.

Be True to Yourself

If you know where you want to go, get an accurate map and follow the directions without compromise. To do otherwise is not being true to your objective. Similarly, if you want to enjoy the benefits of the marital relationship, apply the time-proven BBI map to ensure a marital relationship that is complete, consistent, and holy (set apart for God) in all areas of life.

In addition to the BBI, there are many time-proven truths relative to vocation, health, interpersonal relationships, money, time management, and the like. These truths must be practiced faithfully to enjoy life in whatever form it shows itself. The objective is to enjoy the Marital Dance to the limits of your talents and capabilities. That objective is impossible outside the practice of time-verified truth.

To be true, avoid lies your emotions tell you. Indeed, the ultimate folly is to allow your emotions dictate truth outside of reason. If your emotions rule outside of truth, you will make critical decisions that will result in faulty, harmful results. In plain words, that is stupid.

Consider the lesson of King Solomon, who wrote the book of Proverbs (which demonstrates he knew the truth). Consequently, he was known as a wise man. However, he believed the lie that he could violate that truth and still win. As such, Solomon was not true to God, not true to himself, and not true to those who trusted him.

Similarly, the divorce courts are full of people who thought they could beat God's laws of cause and effect. Truth is law with consequences; it is not open to human manipulation. If you ignore the truth, you will suffer a double whammy: a) loss of the benefits of truth, and b) the inherent consequences of misapplied or faulty truth.

For intuitive application: *outside of truth, you lose.*

4. Making Valid Decisions

Good decision-making is fundamental to a happy, enduring Marital Dance. A marital relationship involves two people who compound the need for and difficulty in making valid decisions. However, if the two are as one, they should be able to make optimum decisions in minimum time and with minimal potential for error.

At times, a couple will find themselves in turbulent waters, as suggested in the photo below. The turbulent waters might be due to mental illness, unfaithfulness, addiction, lack of self-control, abuse, and the like. It can be difficult to make critical decisions even when in calm waters. When in turbulent waters, when the emotions are high and time is limited, valid decision-making becomes problematic. Yet when in turbulent waters, you must be able to make timely, valid decisions to avoid severe consequences, even unto death.

For example, when my wife and I were canoeing, we experienced life-threatening turbulence due to terrain, high water, and wind. In those conditions, the ability to make good, valid decisions was critical to life. Teamwork was paramount for safety. My wife, in the front seat of the canoe, had the responsibility to lead us on the safest route through the rapids. I was in the rear seat, responsible for steering the canoe according to my wife's instructions. The ability to give and follow instructions was critical.

We experienced no major accidents, but our teamwork was often tested. We were running rapids that should have been no problem. We were enjoying the thrill when my wife saw a submerged boulder that showed little surface evidence of its location and potential danger. With little time to react, she yelled, "To the right, to the right!" I thought she meant to head the canoe to the right, and so I did. We hit the only rock in the middle of the rapids—head-on.

Fortunately, no serious damage was done, but that mistake could have been serious in more turbulent waters. To avoid that situation, my wife led with her paddle rather than her voice. I followed her paddle-lead accordingly.

To the extent possible, when in calm waters, plan, so you know what to do when in turbulent waters. Practicing in calm waters saved our lives on several occasions when the waters suddenly turned turbulent in response to raging winds.

This section will focus on a method to make critical decisions based on reason outside the influence of emotion. After a decision is made, concentrate on ways to make the desired results happen.

Decision-Making When in the Turbulent Waters of Life

Making Critical Decisions

We will make some of the most critical and difficult decisions when we are in turbulent waters. A wrong decision can mean death. In calm waters, life continually presents us with options that require the ability to make wise decisions—to buy or not to buy, literally and metaphorically. To make wise decisions requires knowledge and discernment. One must recognize when right shifts to wrong, when wants override needs, or when emotion overtakes reason in the final buy decision. The wisdom in those decisions will determine the nature of the benefits or consequences.

An example of when right can shift to wrong in decision-making is when one chooses to go into debt for an item that is *nice but unnecessary*. If the debt burden is difficult to service, it is foolish (wrong) to even consider buying a nice but unnecessary item with increased debt. To reduce stress, reduce your debt burden. Don't fill your mind with wants beyond needs.

Relative to the evils of debt, my father, who suffered through the Great Depression of the 1930s, noted that the rewards of debt are sweet at first but bitter when the time comes to pay up. With no "up" to pay "down," we lost our home.

Often, the analysis yields several viable alternatives. Which car, church, college, insurance policy, mate, or job is best for us? For example, assume you are in the final stages of house shopping. You have narrowed it down to three options. How do you make the optimum decision without letting your emotions or biases dominate? For such critical decisions, apply a relatively simple procedure I call the *Credit Selection Process*.

The Credit Selection Process

Alternatives		!	HOUSE A	!	HOUSE B	!	HOUSE C
Considerations	Value	Rating	Credits	Rating	Credits	Rating	Credits
Near School	5 x	4 =	20	9	45	3	15
Cost/Value	8	8	64	8	64	3	24
Near Park	7	6	42	7	49	6	42
Near Church	4	2	08	7	28	8	32
Near Parents	8	4	32	5	40	9	72
Family Fit	9	8	72	7	63	5	45
Neighborhood	8	6	48	5	40	5	40
Sidewalks	1	10	10	6	06	0	00
Total Credits→ Relative Value			296 88%		335 100%		270 80%

There are two components in the Credit Selection Process: the *alternatives* or options (houses A, B, and C) and the *considerations* (all the areas of interest). The considerations vary in relative value. A value of 10 indicates the highest worth; a 1 indicates the lowest value, barely a consideration. Assign a rating to each alternative for a given consideration and relative to each other. A rating of 10 indicates the highest contribution; a 1 indicates little to no value.

After assigning values and ratings, multiply the value times the rating to yield the subcredit. Add the subcredits to determine the net credits for that house. The house with the most credits is the logical choice. To make good decisions, you want a wide spread between the top contenders. To get a wider spread, repeat the analysis of houses A and B with greater detail in the considerations. Repeat these refinements until you are satisfied that the entire process (not the results) fairly represents the needs and wants of you and your spouse.

The Credit Selection Process is also an excellent communication tool for learning the desires and needs of your mate. It may be beneficial for you and your mate to make independent evaluations and compare the results to see where your differences lie. My wife and I used the process with great benefit, since we were both involved in the decision-making. It is also helpful for making critical decisions for and with your children. To help them maintain integrity, guide them through the process. Since they are party to the decision-making, they are more likely to accept the results as their own. You do not have to push your value system on them. All are happy.

Most of the turbulent waters of life have hidden snares that can complicate good decision-making. For example, decisions are easily made on Sunday: "I am going to start studying, saving, exercising, whatever *tomorrow*." The critical test of that simplistic decision-making starts tomorrow, on Monday.

To make it happen, employ Enforcers:

- Mental and Spiritual Preparation
- Self-Analysis of Strengths and Weaknesses
- Accountability (to self and others)
- Rewards and Punishment
- Plan and Analysis
- Advice and Counsel

Mental Enforcers

(The following definitions are paraphrased from Merriam-Webster.)

Discernment *is the ability to comprehend what is accurate, correct, and suitable.*

    Discernment helps to determine when it is appropriate to give or withhold criticism.

    Discernment helps to recognize the poison hidden in a decision that appears innocent.

Discrimination *is the ability to select what is accurate, appropriate, and excellent.*

    We can *discriminate* between good and evil by studying their long-term effects.

Perception *implies quick, sympathetic discernment.*

    A Marital Dance of excellence requires in-depth *perception* of the BBI.

Penetration *implies a searching mind that goes beyond what is obvious or superficial.*

    Our *penetration* into the BBI gives us appreciation for its brilliance in application.

Insight *suggests discernment with understanding.*

    The practice of the BBI comes naturally from the *insight* gained by study and application.

Acumen *implies characteristic penetration combined with keen practical judgment.*

    Their marital success is due to their *acumen* and practice of biblical basics.

Determination *involves a firm, fixed, and stubborn mindset focused on the desired result.*

    Despite social pressures, her *determination* to support her husband never wavered.

Integrity *is a determined practice of moral and ethical values.*

    Integrity is rooted in honesty and truth; it is complete and incorruptible.

    Integrity is the most treasured gift you can give your mate.

Courage *is the ability to uphold moral conviction in dangerous and difficult situations.*

    Courage can take many forms, as described by the following synonyms:

        Mettle suggests staying power under adverse conditions.

        Spirit suggests a temperament to maintain high morale even when opposed.

    Resolution stresses firm determination to achieve prescribed goals.

    Tenacity implies stubborn persistence and unwillingness to quit.

To ensure the desired results, remember:

Valid Decision-Making and Making the Decision Valid
Are Foundational to an Enjoyable Marital Dance.
So Let Us Plan to Make It Happen.

5. Planning

Often in life, what we see can be conflicting, as illustrated in the following photo (which is unaltered). Should we play in the snow, work the garden, or pray for wisdom to do the right? All three choices are critical to planning. Conflict is inevitable if one mate sees snow and the other sees blooming flowers. Conflict does not make for good planning. Lack of good planning does not make for a happy marriage.

Planning: Play in the Snow, Work the Garden, or Pray?

The reality is that two people who differ mentally, physically, and spiritually are united in the confines called marriage. Those two different people can see the same scene from the perspective of different needs. That reality is seedbed to a swarm of potential evils that have their roots in values, lifestyle, faith, expectations, and more.

A nasty evil in the group is called *expectations*. We say the traditional "I do" with the expectation that our mate will do for us what we envision or have experienced. For example, my daughter tells the story of a couple with conflicting expectations based on their past experiences. The wife expected her new husband to carry out the trash and perform related duties. The husband saw that work as the duty of his new wife. Consequently, the tasks were left undone to the consternation of both mates. They required professional counseling to help resolve the issue.

My wife and I are fortunate to have enjoyed a reasonable level of unity in our relationship and decision-making. We wanted to keep it that way. Indeed, we wanted to preserve and enhance the rhythm, grace, beauty, and harmony we enjoyed in our Marital Dance. To meet that need, we devised the M-12 (Mission-12) plan, which is essentially a family board meeting. (I heard the term Mission-12 in church, but I do not know its origin or application. I use the term because it fits the purpose.)

Following is an outline of our M-12 meetings, which we practiced with significant benefit to our marital relations. Take what works, modify as needed, apply, and then enjoy.

Mission-12 Meeting Objectives

- Discuss, adjust, and confirm goals and objectives to current realities
  (faith, finances, family values, and lifestyle)
- Make plans for next year's vacations, purchases, trips, etc.
- Develop and agree upon next year's budget
- Identify and address potential problem areas
- Discuss ways and means to strengthen our marriage and improve family relations
- Discuss concerns and unfulfilled expectations that could become divisive
- Address critical problems before they have time to fester and poison the marital body (*nip it in the bud* before it becomes a major problem)

What, When, and Where

We usually held our M-12 sessions at the end of the year in a pleasant, relaxing setting such as a state park lodge. The friendly setting helped to ensure success in a nonstressful environment.

Budgeting

A common marital problem is a lack of financial planning. Bills are due and there's no money to pay, resulting in stress and marital discord.

> "If you had not bought that dress, we would have the money to pay our bills."
> "Oh no, I needed that dress for work. You didn't need that new golf driver. You are
> the spender in this family. Don't blame me for your spendthrift ways."

Note the double fault: there is no money to pay the bills. That reality is also adversely affecting their priceless marital harmony. Few marriages can continue under those stress conditions repeated in various forms throughout the year.

To minimize that destructive potential, a major priority of our M-12 sessions was financial planning, as in preparing and agreeing on a budget. The objective was a balanced budget—allocating our income to ensure it was sufficient for present and future needs. To ensure a balanced budget at the end of the year, we developed and agreed on enforcement measures to ensure the desired results.

We know couples who do not budget or discipline their spending to the realities of their income. They suffer self-inflicted stress supported by many reasons why they *do not* budget. Reality curbs their spending into a kind of false budget that enables them to survive but with no hope for a better tomorrow. Those realities suggested a philosophy that helped us make and keep a budget.

Our guiding philosophy: *regardless of the size of our income, we will survive; we will not starve or freeze to death.* (This philosophy assumed no conditions beyond our control, such as war or natural disasters). Survival adrenaline would kick in to save us. By necessity, we would adjust our cash outflow to the realities of our income (if you do not have it, you can't spend it.) That reality dictated our behavior. When the limits of credit and the goodwill of friends are reached, we have two options: adjust or perish.

To make it happen, we developed a budget that anticipated and covered all but the abnormal hazards of life. For inspiration, we kept this saying in mind: "Good sailors prepare for rough seas and hazards; foolish sailors assume calm seas."

Noble sentiments are easily voiced on Sunday when the sun is shining and the birds are singing. However, the realities of Monday will test our mettle. To budget and hold to that budget requires a disciplined mindset. So let's review the main reasons to budget and how to ensure success.

Some Christians take issue with budgeting and planning. They note that the Bible teaches that we should not be anxious about our lives, for the God who cares for the sparrow will take care of us (see Mat 6:25, 26). Ergo, planning and budgeting are unnecessary. Indeed, they show a lack of faith in the promise of God to provide.

In reply, such verses should be viewed and evaluated in the context of all scripture. If we interpreted that passage from Matthew literally, we would all perish. When I plant a seed, build a house, or do any of the deeds for survival, I am taking thought for tomorrow.

From another perspective, God provided the sunshine, rain, fertile soil, and seeds that can reproduce more than a hundredfold. He then gave us the precious gifts of mind and muscle to create, do, and harvest. God has done His part and more. Likewise, we need to do our part. As for the sparrows, God provided the seeds; the sparrow has to do its part to find the seeds.

So why budget? An overriding reason to budget is to ensure that your lifestyle is within the realities of your income. A secondary reason relates to the realities of life that show periods of plenty and periods of want, as illustrated by Joseph in the book of Genesis, who reaped from seven years of plenty to cover seven years of famine.

Another reason for budgeting is the fantastic growth benefits over time, as described in Insurance Measure 2 on Excellence. In the following, we will review the compounded potential benefits of a budget based on the rigors of math (detailed in Appendix III). For ease of understanding, the math is rounded off and simplified. Still, for many, the math will be new, without meaning. If such is your case, know that the math and the Bible support the same process and resultant conclusions. You can apply the process with confidence.

In the following, we will illustrate the incredible benefits of a budget by example. Consider the growth potential of $100 saved per week over a marital lifespan of forty-two years. One hundred dollars per week equals $5,000 per year (50 work weeks/year x $100/week = $5,000). If you buried your savings, you would have $210,000 saved at the end of forty-two years—not too shabby.

However, if you invested the saved money at a nominal growth rate of 5 percent, you would have over three times as much: $676,000. If you studied and averaged a 10 percent growth rate, in line with the stock market average over the last fifty years, you would have $2,680,000 in your account. If you studied diligently and invested wisely, achieving an average return of 15 percent per annum, you would have more than $11,700,000 in your account—with only $210,000 of that amount being the money you earned and saved.

To average a 15 percent annual growth rate (generally) requires an astute, disciplined investor who daily checks the status of the investments and market climate. Market timing is also critical. From 2012 to 2021, the market averaged a return of almost 15 percent per annum. When I studied one hour per workday and spent several evenings a month reviewing the stock market, I averaged 15 percent too. When I didn't research and daily check the market, I could and did go negative. Over the last twenty years, I have averaged an 8 percent growth rate. That means my investment doubled every nine years. It is like tending your garden. It can yield from zero to a hundredfold, dependent upon the degree of your care and attention.

The above illustrates the fantastic value (blessings) of compounded time. Most of that potential will be lost in the absence of a disciplined budget. For personal application, the same math applies to talents, knowledge, health, and the like. The lesson: nourish your God-given talents to enjoy the compounded, bountiful blessings that flow consequently.

Math also has a negative side that shows its horrible face when the investment goes sour, as when a destructive force ruins your garden. Assume you invest $5,000 and lose half of it during a market decline. After the loss comes the horrible aftershock: you have lost 50 percent, and it will require a 100 percent return to regain your original $5,000. That 100 percent will, on average, require one doubling period. At the nominal 10 percent annual rate of return experienced by the stock market, seven years will pass before you regain the original amount.

The lesson: you can prepare a garden, and you may lose part or all of it by flood, vandalism, disease, insects, drought, frost, and more. So why garden?

In response, it is a certainty that if you don't prepare a garden, the fertile soil and the rains will be of no benefit to you. You will have no harvest and will suffer the consequences of empty shelves over a cold, harsh winter. However, if you put in a garden and work it properly, you will generally enjoy a bountiful harvest to carry you through the winter.

Investing is similar. If you invest conservatively, under normal conditions, you will enjoy the average rate of return—about 10 percent per year over the past forty to fifty years.

The plus and minus sides of investment math apply to biblical blessings. Consistent practice of God's ways, of law and order, will benefit from the positive side and avoid the horrible consequence of the negative side. Consistent practice pays big dividends toward survival, even in times of war, famine, and the like.

To become a wise investor, review the math, read books on investment, and invest conservatively until positive results are under your belt. Before you invest your savings, make sure you understand and apply the following four principles that have their roots in the math. Note that these principles also apply toward enjoying a full and abundant marital life.

Four Principles of Investing

1. *Effective use of time* is critical to enjoying benefits (money, talents, whatever) at retirement. If you can get one extra doubling period by saving early or saving wisely, your net worth will be twice the amount of the previous doubling period. From another perspective, the first doubling period will net you one dollar per dollar saved. The same amount of time in the sixth doubling period will earn you $32 for every dollar saved. For emphasis: to enjoy the growth benefits, start a savings program as soon after your conception as possible.

2. *Extra effort* has incredible compounding benefits. For example, assume that your parents gave you a wedding gift of $20,000 (the average cost of a wedding in 2020). Of that amount, you saved half ($10,000) for retirement. Forty-two years later, on your wedding anniversary, you would have $10,000 if you stored the money in a coffee can. If you invested that money at an average return of 5 percent per year, you would have about $77,600; at 10 percent, $550,000; and at 15 percent, $3,540,000.

   Of significance, the first 5 percent gain nets you about $67,000—not too bad. However, the added 5 percentage points from 10 percent to 15 percent will earn you about three million dollars. That is dramatic support for going the extra mile in your marital relationship and decision-making.

   The lesson: *for maximum gain and benefit, give life your best.*

3. *Avoid the terrible consequences of losses:*
   - Monitor and protect your nest egg (savings)
   - Let your gains run; cut your losses short
   - Never borrow for nonessentials

4. *Time defines life.* To earn money takes the time that defines your life. As such, money, time, and life are interrelated and interdependent. That means that if you spend money foolishly, you are foolishly wasting your life. With that perspective, treat money as an extension of your life, for so it is.

For application of the above, imagine you have a gaggle of geese that regularly lay golden eggs, which become golden geese. Each golden goose you sell or lose will no longer produce golden eggs that can become golden goslings. It will require a significant amount of time for the remaining golden geese to replace the lost or stolen geese. Wisdom encourages you to guard your geese with your life—for you bought them with money that requires time that defines your life. Now your golden geese provide means to sustain and improve your life.

There is a caution light: to minimize economic stress potential, increase your number of golden geese. However, there is a point where more golden geese come at a considerable cost to your time and your marital relationship. For that reason, the Bible encourages moderation in your getting. Biblically and realistically, it is foolish to build ever-greater barns, to house more geese beyond need, at the expense of a solid relationship with God, family, and friends. Similarly, it is foolish to waste time and resources going into winter's barren realities with empty barns—no geese.

The mathematically based lessons apply to all areas of life. The math supports the biblical precepts that encourage us to give our best to enjoy life to the limits of our talents. To reap a bountiful harvest of blessings, we have only to know and practice His ways. When we practice His ways, *we do not have to be concerned about or give thought to tomorrow.*

Preparing a Budget

My wife asked this critical question: "Why can't we adjust our standard of living to our income, as do many of your fellow workers?" To answer that question, my wife and I had a financial planning session. We laid out our future needs and desires, the standard of living we wanted, fixed expenditures, income, and more. We both agreed that a basic priority was to save for a down payment on a house. We knew there would never be a down payment unless we took steps to make it happen—by way of a budget.

There are many budgeting plans. By design, we wanted our budget to be simple to maintain and ensure the desired results.

To start the budgeting process, we divided our income into two funds: *Reserve* and *Cash Flow.*

The *Reserve Fund* was designed to cover present and future needs (house payments, taxes, insurance, savings for retirement, car repair and replacement, special needs, major purchases, vacation, emergencies, and other). The *Cash Flow Fund* consisted of our net income minus the Reserve Fund. Our standard of living was defined by these two funds.

To ensure a *balanced budget*, we agreed to the following:
- We would not go into debt except for a home, health, and (possibly) business.
- We would walk, eat beans, and do whatever necessary to ensure a balanced budget.

The advantage of this budget is simplicity. For daily spending, we limited ourselves to the realities of the Cash Flow Fund. If money ran out, we agreed to do without or downsize. By agreement, I got a weekly allowance for my needs and expenses. The remaining money in the Cash Flow Fund was under my wife's control. To her credit, she kept within the confines of the budget—except at Christmas, when she occasionally exceeded budget.

Benefits of the M-12 Meetings
- The potentially harmful effects of marital problems were minimized.
     Nip it in the bud before it grows.
- We enjoyed both the short and long-term benefits of a balanced budget.
     We never had a problem or dispute relative to financial matters.
     There was always money for critical needs.
- We enjoyed our Marital Dance because we took measures to ensure, maintain,
     and enhance our marital relationship and dancing skills.

Chapter 6
Exemplars

It is an interesting observation: when a task is declared impossible, it tends to be impossible. To some people, a wall is not necessarily a solid barrier. By God's help, it can be conquered. In religious circles, we call these people *saints*. Relative to the Marital Dance, we call them *exemplars*. Exemplars show that the impossible is possible and even doable. To the exemplars, the perceived solid wall is only a disguised gate. The challenge is to find a way to go over, under, around, or through the gate. The exemplar provides hope to those confined behind a gate perceived to be an impenetrable wall.

Consider: before 1954, running a four-minute mile (at an average rate of fifteen miles per hour for the distance of one mile) was perceived as a limit until Roger Bannister showed it could be done. According to Wikipedia, from the time Bannister exceeded that limit in 1954 until April 2021, 1,663 athletes ran the "impossible" mile in less than four minutes. Further, the record was broken by a significant margin of seventeen seconds. To those runners, Roger Bannister served as an exemplar of how to do the improbable. What did he eat? What was his training schedule and routine? What set him apart from his peers?

Fortunately, in our faith, we have the ultimate exemplar in our Lord, Jesus Christ. Therefore, to be effective, my behavior should conform to the ways He taught and lived. However, Christ had a unique mission: He was more than a mortal and never married. Accordingly, my mental, physical, and spiritual impossibilities were not the same for Christ. To satisfy that reality, I find it helpful to have inspirational exemplars who share my human frailties.

Exemplars are where you find them. Horses are exemplary for their servitude. Dogs are exemplary for their faithfulness. Daffodils are exemplary for their smiling faces, even in adversity, when snow covers their bodies and their peers are still sleeping. In contrast, cows are at the low end of the exemplar scale, not in the same class as horses, dogs, or daffodils. My father didn't know that. He bought a Guernsey cow and gave me the responsibility of caring for our new family member, Daisy. (Oh Lord, why a cow? I had prayed for a pony.) Unbelievably, our lowly cow was a daily exemplar of the ways and behavior of a saint. She returned good for evil, was content, gave generously, held no grudges, and made the most of what she had. I recall no incident when Daisy showed any but saintly behavior. She gave her best without reservation. From a behavioral perspective, she was the only saint in our family.

At that time, I did not appreciate my good fortune. I had been given the task of caring for a common cow. In turn, I was cared for and raised by a saint. How wondrous Your ways, oh Lord! I prayed for a pony; you provided a saint as a playmate, provider, and exemplar.

As you give, so shall you receive. Daisy not only provided, but she also received. When our family could no longer care for an animal, it usually went to the stockyards or the butcher. Because of her meritorious service and behavior, Daisy received deserving consideration. I never saw her abused by any family member. When we could no longer care for her, my father considered her worthy of a noble end in line with her noble character. So Daisy ended her days on a nearby farm and not as a number in the stockyards. (For further details, see my brother Harry's article, "Remembering Daisy," published in *Country Magazine*, April/May 2009).

As noted above and in the Bible, our Lord instructed by way of the unexpected. Who would have the Lord of Lords be born in a stable to an ordinary couple and welcomed by common shepherds? Who would think of a cow as an exemplar of saintly behavior? Similarly, who would think of a coon as an exemplar of *determination* and *persistence,* prime virtues in an enduring marital dance?

We have peach trees. When the peaches are almost ripe, the coons move in and have peach parties—more like drunken brawls, judging from the results. After one of their parties, the area around the peach trees is a mess—torn leaves, limbs, and peaches laid waste. To save peaches, I trapped the coons in a cage guaranteed to hold any coon.

One evening, I checked the cage and noted a coon in a submissive position, as if it had already given up—there was no way out. Surprisingly, the next morning, my coon-proof cage was empty. I had caught a "dumb" coon who didn't know his cage was coon-proof. The coon reasoned, "If I got in, I can get out." That coon tore the cage apart trying to find a weakness—and so he did. Because of his persistence, this dumb coon was free. I applauded him for his effort and exemplary lesson. By being an exemplar of *persistence,* the coon also benefited: he lived.

We can find exemplary couples for both do and don't behaviors in marriage. My parents served as negative exemplars: don't do this, or you will suffer the consequences. We can also learn from the many divorces. Why did a marriage, seemingly made in heaven, go sour? Similarly, how did a couple manage to enjoy each other despite their differences?

Exemplars are born when things go wrong. Consider a notable case told to me by my son-in-law, who attended Columbia Bible College. (Additional detail is available from multiple sources on the internet.)

In 1990, President Robertson McQuilkin of Columbia Bible College (now Columbia International University) bewildered his peers by announcing his resignation. The reason: his wife had Alzheimer's disease and needed his full-time attention.

His resignation seemed to defy reason. Certainly, his talents were needed and better utilized in the formation and development of young minds. Certainly, a trained caretaker could better provide for his wife's needs than he could. As a caretaker, he would be involved with personal care, including the intimate realities of incontinence. The everyday realities of personal care compared to the prestige and privileges of the office of the president evoke the question: Why?

From his interviews and speeches, it appears that his decision to resign from his prestigious position started with his marriage vow to care for and be one with his wife in sickness, health, plenty, or want. His wife cared for him while climbing the ladder to the office of college president. Now his wife was in need. It was his time to respond in kind, and so he did.

Still, the question lingers: Why?

President McQuilkin's decision was and is inspirational. In their marriage vows, he and his wife Muriel committed to each other for life. My wife and I made similar vows to be one with each other—regardless. She fulfilled her vow and more when I was physically disabled. When my turn came to do likewise, would I be willing to serve her personal needs?

My wife was in a severe auto accident that resulted in a broken neck. Thanks to skilled hands, she is not paralyzed, but she is a semi-invalid, requiring personal and, at times, intimate care. Now comes the unexpected part, consequential to our vows to become one. She and I are one, and so the care I give her is not a chore. I care for her the same way I care for my own personal injury or ill health. As I want to ease my pain and misery, I likewise desire to ease her pain and suffering resulting from her injuries. In Unity, our pains and joys are mutual.

Exemplars of agape love make it easier to become one with and serve our mates. Some two thousand years ago, the One called the Messiah, the Lord of Lords, stooped and washed the feet of His followers. He advised us to follow His lead. As noted above, President McQuilkin became an exemplar of Christ's teachings. He gave up a prestigious position to become a servant to another, willingly performing the most intimate of tasks. As demonstrated by his works, agape love has no limits.

In contrast, we are challenged by a pervasive worldview: "Don't be confined by the constraints of others. Do your thing and enjoy." This invitation is appealing, but it has little to no merit in application. Consider: we enter the Marital Dancewith little knowledge and no experience. Accordingly, it is foolish to expect to enjoy that critical Marital Dance based on ignorance. Indeed, *do your thing* (in ignorance) and be prepared to *suffer the consequences*. In contrast, wisdom says to learn and benefit from the experience of past dancers—good and bad. To gain from their experience, find exemplars who showed how they succeeded in marriage or why they lost.

When certain behaviors appear enticing, find exemplars of that behavior. What is their winning record? Interestingly, I could find no models who consistently violated the BBI and won. If exemplars of wisdom and stature couldn't (such as Solomon, David, and former president Clinton), what chance do you or I have of winning while practicing their failed ways?

In response to the above, wisdom says:

> To win and enjoy the Marital Dance for Life,
>> know and practice the time-proven ways and means of the dance
>>> as detailed in the BBI and practiced by its exemplars.

Chapter 7
Fourteen Steps

Toward a Joyful Marital Dance

The Stairway of Life

The photo symbolically represents marital life that is taken one step at a time, up or down. Each step can take you up to ethereal highs (marriage at its finest) or down to the pits (marriage at its worst). To enjoy or not enjoy depends on your direction—up or down. To ensure marriage at its best and enjoy the euphoria at the top of the staircase, look up and keep climbing. For inspiration, focus on and copy the ways of the exemplars (noted in Chapter 6) who reached the top and consequently enjoyed marriage to the max. If they can do it, so can we—one small step upward at a time. The view at the top is worth the effort. At the top, the woes of the valley from which you came are inconsequential.

Following are Fourteen Steps that lead to the top of the Stairway, where marriage is at its finest. Note that each step starts with an action *do* verb (*be, secure, make,* and so on).

Critical Steps:

1. ***Be Dedicated Christians***
   Shared faith is foundational to maintaining Unity in a marital relationship.
   Practiced faith is foundational toward enjoying an enduring Marital Dance.

2. ***Secure the Marriage in the Courtship Dance***
   Select a potential mate who complements your bent and supports your core values.
   Save sexual intimacy for the Marital Dance.

3. ***Be True to God, Yourself, and Your Mate***
   Truth starts with God, as revealed in the Biblical Behavioral Instructions (BBI).
   The BBI have no virtue unless correctly applied and practiced.

4. ***Be Fit Mentally, Physically, and Spiritually***
   Fitness is conformance to a set of time-proven behavioral standards (such as the BBI).
   Marital fitness defines your level of marital joy.

5. ***Make a Lifetime Commitment to be One with Your God and Your Mate***
   Give Unity the value and sanctity of life. Infidelity destroys Unity.
   Agape love is foundational to maintaining Unity (as detailed in 1 Cor 13).

6. ***Establish Goals and Objectives***
   Dance as one toward a common goal. Stay focused.
   Know where you are going and why.

7. ***Maintain a Can-Do Attitude***
   Chunk it and blitz it. You can through Christ
   In contrast, when you think "I can't," it is final—*you can't*.

8. ***Maximize Benefits in Your Marital Dance***
   Maintain balance in all areas: mental, physical, and spiritual.
   Prioritize. Focus on the critical A tasks; do the noncritical C tasks as time permits.
   Finish the task in conformance with Pareto's 80/20 principle.

9. ***Avoid Problems and Errors***
   Identify and correct potential problems before they become major.
   To permanently resolve a problem, eliminate the cause(s).
   To avoid errors, *be true* and *be sure* before you act.

10. ***Recognize and Respect the Behavioral Fence***
    The Behavioral Fence defines the divide between beneficial and harmful behaviors.
    The BBI defines the Behavioral Fence by identifying beneficial and harmful behaviors.
    To enjoy the Marital Dance, give the Behavioral Fence distance.

11. ***Ensure Enduring Joy in Your Marriage***
    Don't assume. Know, plan, and do, and then monitor, maintain, and improve.
    Periodically test for marital fitness and adjust accordingly.

12. ***Hold Periodic Planning Sessions***
    Identify weaknesses for correction and strengths for growth.
    Enhance the marital relationship by planning activities and projects.
    Ensure financial fitness by implementing a budget.

13. ***Improve toward Excellence***
    Excellence results from the effective practice of mind and time management.
    Do it right the first time; do it better the next time.

14. ***Dance Magnificently and Always with Joy***
    Dance consistently, effortlessly, and intuitively.

"Tis a gift to be simple,
Tis a gift to be free."

(from a Shaker folk song by J. Merman)

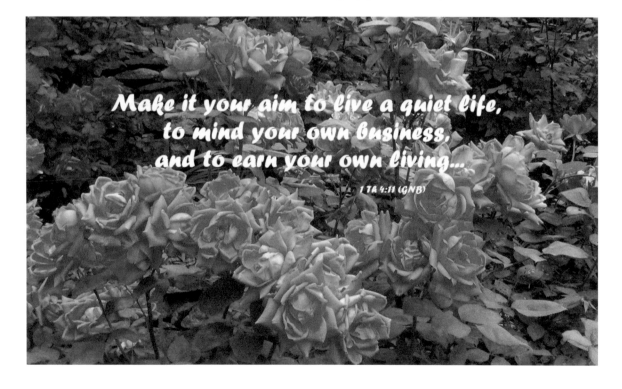

Make it your aim to live a quiet life,
to mind your own business,
and to earn your own living...

1 TA 4:11 (GNB)

Appendix I
The Biblical Behavioral
Instructions (BBI)

Marriage defines life, which can vary from levels of joy and euphoria to despair and death. Except for nuanced situations, the joys and sorrows experienced in marriage are self-induced by what we do and don't do. Wisdom says to do what is time-proven to produce the desired results. Fortunately, those needs are met by the BBI, which come with impeccable, time-tested credentials. The BBI cover all areas of life, including time, money, and mind management; conflict resolution; decision-making; and more. The BBI are final, complete, and ultimate. When it comes to ensuring marital harmony, the BBI have no peer. You can practice the BBI with confidence since the desired results are time-proven to be consequential to the behavior.

In application, there is a problem. The BBI are spread in a book comprised of sixty-six minibooks that include theology and history. There is duplication, redundancy, and antiquated words. Accordingly, as shown by the *Barna Reports*, most Christians do not take the time to study the Bible as required to become familiar with and practice God's ways. A condensed version of the BBI is needed as a reference for daily application in the marital relationship. From that need is born the BBI detailed in this appendix

The Bible has many interpretations in the theology of the Jewish and Christian faiths. However, when it comes to behavior, the Bible is clear, concise, and thorough on what we should and should not do to enjoy life and our marital relationships. To prepare the BBI, I outlined the Bible (King James Version, or KJV) several times, focusing on the New Testament. Then I pulled all references to behavior. The result was lengthy, with obsolete English words, duplications, and redundancies.

I reviewed a given verse in some twenty versions to reduce, simplify, and get a good understanding. I then reduced the verses to key words and thoughts. In the process, I changed obsolete words (thees, thous, etc.) to modern English forms. I removed duplications and phrases not directly applicable to a marital relationship. I took the most relevant ideas and paraphrased the verses to make them simpler and more useful as a reference and guide. In all cases, I was careful to stay within the context of the verse as commonly portrayed in the various translations.

The abbreviated verse citation shown is identified with the version that served as its base or to which it is most closely aligned: e.g., Joh 3:16 CEV. If no version is given, the default version is the Modern King James Version, or MKJV. To readily identify the paraphrased text as being biblical, the verse(s) will be italicized.

As a point of interest, most versions of the Bible essentially say the same thing in different dialects and with different emphasis. For example, eight versions have the same wording as the KJV in Exodus 20:15: "Thou shalt not steal." Variations include "Never steal," "You are not to steal," and "Thou dost not steal."

To maintain their sanctity and purity, the BBI are presented with minimal comments. Read, study, and apply them to your marital bent and needs. Toward voluntary and disciplined practice, evaluate each biblical instruction (the cause) relative to the desired consequences (the effects).

The BBI relate to the dance music (agape love), choreography, and behavior. To gain insight into shades of meaning and application for words such as *dissipation, vileness, holiness, godliness,* and *submission,* reference a dictionary, concordance, or Bible commentary. For in-depth study, cross-reference the verse in several translations and commentaries.

When you understand that the BBI are beneficial and reliable, you no longer have to comply; you want to know, apply, and conform. That is the objective: voluntary, intuitive practice. The BBI are gems of wisdom that show a picture of an ideal person or mate as envisioned by our Creator. In time, that image can fade or become distorted. To renew the image, to be inspired to improve, and to discover subtle areas for improvement, review the BBI periodically.

As tenets of faith, *the BBI have no merit outside of knowing and faithful practice.*

★★★

Faith

Sharing a common faith is fundamental to enjoying an enduring marital relationship. Accordingly, this book assumes that the couple is married and shares a common Christian faith. If you or your mate are not Christian, there are many books on becoming a Christian, such as *Foundations for Your Faith* by D. J. Kennedy. The New Testament is foundational to why and how to become a Christian. The four-step process to enjoy the ways of our Creator is summarized in 2 Chronicles 7:14:

> *If my people, which are called by my name, shall (1) humble themselves, (2) pray, (3) seek my face and (4) turn from their wicked ways; then will I forgive their sin and heal their land.*

Christianity is confirmed by willing compliance to the ways of Christ: *I will show you my faith from my works. If it does not have works, faith is dead.* —James 2:14–20

Basics

Seek first the kingdom of God and His righteousness.	—Mat 6:33
Do it all for the glory of God.	—1 Cor 10:31
Be *transformed by the renewing of your mind.*	—Rom 12:2

Repent, Believe, and be Baptized

The old lifestyle is characterized by *sin* (un-Quality)	
All wrongdoing is sin.	—1 John 5:17 GNB
If you fail to do what you know is right, you are sinning.	—James 4:17 RVV
To change: *Repent* (recognize past errors), *believe* (know and accept a better way) and *be baptized* (wash out the old, be cleansed, and let the new control.)	
Repent and be baptized for the forgiveness of your sins.	—Acts 2:38 ESV

Agape Love

Agape love works toward the good of your mate, independent of their merit. Agape love is the music that suggests behavior that contributes to an enjoyable, lifetime Marital Dance. Agape love is the magic elixir that holds a marriage together under all but the most extreme cases (involving mental, physical, or spiritual disorders that require special counsel outside the scope of this book).

It is difficult to imagine divorce between mates who practice agape love per the following:

Love comes from a pure heart, a good conscience, and a sincere faith.	—1 Tim 1:5
If I speak with the tongues of men and of angels, and have not charity (Agape love)	
I am nothing. Faith, hope, and charity, the greatest of these is charity.	— 1 Cor 13

This (1 Cor 13) is the "Love Chapter." To enhance your marriage and Christian living, read, study, and apply the whole chapter.

If [your mate] strikes you on the right cheek, turn to him [her] the other also.	—Mat 5:39
Do not pay back wrong for wrong, but be [kind] to [your mate].	—1 Th 5:15 GNB

Prayer

Why? *Everyone that asketh receiveth, and he that seeketh findeth.*	—Mat 7:8 KJV
How? *This is how you should pray: Our Father in heaven, hallowed be your name.*	—Mat 6:9-13
When? *Pray continually.*	—1 Th 5:17

Forgiveness

In a marital relationship, you will do wrong to and be wronged by your mate. Given that reality, the art of giving and receiving forgiveness per the BBI is fundamental.

Forgiveness has several levels. At the lowest level, the wronged person voluntarily writes a symbolic note that says *Paid in Full* to the offender (even if the offender is unrepentant). A higher level of forgiveness involves repentance (I admit I did you wrong) and forgiveness (the debt is paid). At the highest level of forgiveness, trust is restored. The receiver of forgiveness (the offender) must be sure that all traces of wrongdoing are corrected to the extent possible. The giver of forgiveness (victim) must have the grace of God never to hold the forgiven, the offender, accountable for the trespass. Trust is restored as if the trespass never occurred. (In extreme cases, make sure that the offender has made inward changes to support their confession.)

In the KJV, there are some forty-eight verses with the word *forgive*. The following are some of those verses.

Forgive us our debts, as we forgive our debtors.	—Mat 6:12
If [your mate] sins against you seven times in the day, and turns to you seven times	
saying, 'I repent,' you must forgive them.	—Luke 17:4
Be merciful as your Father is merciful. Do not judge [condemn].	—Mat 6:14

Freedom

The ultimate freedom: those under godly influence and control can ride the "Winds of the Spirit" to ever-higher levels of full and abundant living—without restriction.

Wherever the Lord's Spirit is, there is freedom.	—2 Cor 3:17 GW
Do not let your freedom make those who are weak fall into sin.	—1 Cor 8:9 GNB

Stay Focused

Whatever you eat, drink, or do; do all for the glory of God.	— 1 Cor 10:31
Add to your faith goodness, knowledge, self-control, perseverance, and godliness.	—2 Pet 1:5, 6
I can do—through Christ.	— Phi 4:13

Commandments

The Great Commandments

All the biblical instructions and guidelines of the BBI have their roots in the Great Commandments. In application, the Great Commandments are positive and dynamic: *do*, as in love.

Jesus was asked, "Which is the greatest commandment in the law?"

Jesus answered:

> *This is the first and great commandment.*
> *You shall love the Lord your God with all your heart, with all your soul, and with all your mind.*
> *The second is similar: You shall love your neighbor as yourself.*
> *On these two commandments hang all the law and the prophets.*   Mat 22:36–40 KJV

(For a treatise on the application and practice of love, reference 1 Cor 13, the Love Chapter.)

The Ten Commandments   *—Exo 20:3–9 and Deut 5:7–21*

The original Ten Commandments were contained on tablets of stone etched by God (Deut 5:22). Practice accordingly. (For insight into the dynamics of the Ten Commandments, reference *The Ten Commandments* by Schlesinger and Vogel.)

1. *You shall have no other Gods before me.*
2. *You shall not make for yourself an idol.*
3. *You shall not misuse the name of your God.*
4. *Remember the Sabbath day by keeping it holy.*
5. *Honor your father and your mother.*
6. *You shall not murder.*
7. *You shall not commit adultery.*
8. *You shall not steal.*
9. *You shall not give false testimony.*
10. *You shall not covet.*

The Golden Rule

> *Jesus said: "Love one another as I have loved you."*   —Jon 13:34

The Great Commission

> *Teach them* [your family] *to observe all that I have commanded you.*   —Mat 28:19, 20 ESV
> Note the emphasis on being complete: to observe *all*.

Behavioral Causes

Our Creator gave us the ability to see, think, create, work, and do. Our Creator also inspired a family of behavioral instructions for our benefit: to enjoy life (your marital relationship), *do this, not that*. The objective is to *want to practice* the BBI from a position of understanding, not blind compliance. Toward understanding and beneficial practice:

- Study the related verses in biblical context. What is each verse saying? What are the inherent benefits of compliance? What are the consequences of noncompliance?

- Look up the definitions of the behavioral words to appreciate the shades of meaning.
- Concentrate on those areas in which you need improvement.

The *do* and *don't* behaviors are not arbitrary or capricious. We obey or face the terrible consequences of misbehavior. As with any game, they are a list of rules for our enjoyment and benefit. To win the game and enjoy, *do this, not that.* To enjoy to the max, know and practice the rules and regulations until they are second nature.

To Benefit:

Show Justice, Mercy, and Faithfulness.	—Mat 23:23
Pursue Righteousness, Endurance, and Gentleness.	—1 Tim 6:11
Be Holy, Compassionate, Humble, Supportive, Forgiving, and Prayerful	—Col 3:12–14,
★ *Think on whatever is— True, Noble, Right, Pure, Lovely, Admirable, Excellent, and Praiseworthy.*	—Phil 4:8
★ *Improve the quality of your Fruit of the Spirit, which is Love, Joy, Peace, Patience, Kindness, Goodness, Faithfulness, Gentleness, and Self-Control.*	—Gal 5:22–23

★ These verses summarize the character of a Quality Christian mate. They are excellent memory gems for daily exercise and practice.

To Avoid Harm, *Don't*

Our behavior defines our lives and marital relationships—for good or evil. To enjoy, concentrate on and master the *do* and avoid the *don't* behaviors. Be careful with nuanced behaviors that can fade from right to wrong or have subtle, long-term, adverse effects such as debt, careless words, and anxiety.

To cover all cases, *be true. Do this and not that.*

(Biblical references are listed at the end.)

Faith-Based Don'ts
   Swearing, Blasphemy, Faithlessness, Unbelief, Idolatry, Witchcraft
Sexual Don'ts
   Immorality, Orgies, Lust, Lewdness, Depravity, Perversion, Fornication, Adultery
Personal Don'ts
   Arrogance, Boasting, Vanity, Insolence, Rudeness, Disrespect, Foolishness, Vileness, Wickedness, Envy, Covetousness, Love of Money, Laziness, Unproductiveness, Debts, Drunkenness, Bitterness, Impurity, Coarse Joking, Evil Thoughts, Debauchery, Cowardice
Social Don'ts
   Theft, Stealing, Greed, Murder, Brutality, Ruthlessness, Rage, Anger, Brawling, Hateful, Malice, Slander, Deceit, Swindling, Strife, Falsehood, Lying, Perjury, Strife, Gossip, Dissensions, Obscenity, Unforgiveness, Disobedience to Parents

(References: Mat 5:34, 12:36; Mark 7:20–22; Luke 21:34; Rom 1:29–31, 3:12–13, 13:8; Eph 4:25, 5:3–5, 5:28–29, 5:31–31, 5:18; Col 3:5, 3:8–9; 1 Tim 1:9–10, 6:10; 2 Tim 2:16, 3:2–3; Titus 3:14; Heb 6:12, 13:5; James 5:12; 1 Pet 4:31; 1 Cor 6:9–10; Gal 5:19–21; Rev 21:8)

Behavioral Instructions

The BBI relate to all areas of life. They guide us through life with the least amount of difficulty and the most joy regardless of circumstances. The purpose of this section is to present biblical guidelines and instructions for daily application and behavior.

Mind Control

Out of the heart come evil thoughts, murder, adultery, immorality, and theft.	—Mat 15:19 ESV
Let each one be fully assured in his mind.	—Rom 14:5
Whatever things are true, honest, right, pure, lovely, and of good report;	
if there is any virtue and if there is any praise, think on these things.	—Phil 4:8

(Phil 4:8 is one of the most important verses toward maintaining a pure, clean mind and changing the Christian life from struggle to enjoyment. A mate of joy is a mate for life.)

Self-Control

Self-control (being disciplined) is the muscle of a marital relationship. To be self-controlled is doing what needs to be done promptly. For maximum benefits, submit your self-control to Master Control.

God did not give us a spirit of timidity, but one of power, love, and self-discipline.	—2 Tim 1:7 ISV
Practice self-control, and keep your minds clear so that you can pray.	—1 Pe 4:7 GW
Know how to live with your wife in a holy and honorable way.	—1 Th 4:4 GNB
Live quietly, mind your own business, and work with your own hands.	—1 Th 4:11 ISV

Discipleship

A disciple consistently and predictably (not necessarily perfectly) performs to the BBI.
Discipleship is Christian faith in action. A mature disciple is the same as a Quality Christian.

Be wise as serpents and as harmless as doves.	—Mat 10:16
All things are lawful for me, but I will not be brought under the power of any.	—1 Cor 6:12
Test everything. Hold on to the good. Avoid every kind of evil.	—1 Th 5:21, 22 ESV
Set an example [for your family]in speech, in life, in love, in faith and in purity.	—1 Tim 4:12
Be quick to listen, slow to speak, and slow to become angry.	—Jas1:19 CEV
Women should display their beauty by dressing modestly and decently, not with elaborate	
hairstyles, or by wearing gold, pearls, or expensive clothes, but through good actions.	—1 Tim 2:9, 10 ISV

The lesson: We are defined by our character, not by our appearance. The most beautiful woman I knew was exterior only. The self-inflicted tragedies of her life give credence to the wisdom in the above verse.

Leadership

In a marital relationship, we are entrusted to uphold God's sacred institution: the family.
To perform the leadership duties of an elder of the family, we should:
- be disciplined and self-controlled;
- be respectable, blameless, and above reproach;
- be a good managers of our families;
- have respectable children of faith;

- be temperate, not given to drunkenness;
- avoid being violent, overbearing, quarrelsome, quick-tempered, or pursuing dishonest gain; and be hospitable. —1 Tim 3:2–4; Titus 1:6–8

In a marital relationship, we have the responsibility to be a servant and attend to the needs of our mates and families. As servants, we should be:

Tested, trustworthy, temperate, worthy of respect, and uphold the truths of our faith. —1 Tim 3:8–11

In addition, we should teach, train, and encourage each other [our mates and families] to—

- *be sound in faith, in love, and in endurance;*
- *not be slanderers, but be pure and kind;*
- *be of sound speech that cannot be condemned; and*
- *be people of integrity.* —Titus 2:2-8

Financial

Some preach a gospel of wealth as a heritage of Christian rights. At the other extreme are vows of poverty taken by some to gain a closer relationship with their God. As we read in the following verses, when God is number 1, the benefits of wealth are secondary.

If we have food and clothing, we will be content.	—1 Tim 6:5–10 ESV
Owe no man anything, except to love each other.	—Rom 13:8 ESV
Give up trying so hard to get rich.	—Prov 23:4 CEV
Excel in the Grace of Giving, for God loves a cheerful giver.	—2 Cor 9:7 KJV

Work and Do

Our Creator gave us the most wondrous gift: the ability to create, work, and do.

The word *work* is mentioned 777 times in the Modern King James Version of the Bible. The word *do* appears 4,709 times, and the word *pray* appears 397 times.

Note the biblical emphasis on working and doing. The emphasis does not negate or degrade prayer. Instead, it indicates that faith (prayer) and works are hand in glove. Caution: the words *work* and *do* have positive and negative connotations in the Bible. You can *do* good and evil *works*.

Work is God-Ordained:
The LORD God put man in the Garden of Eden to work it. —Gen 2:15
Be Skilled and Focused:
She is a hard worker, strong and industrious. —Prov 31:17 GNB
Draw water, strengthen your forts, and [work] the clay. —Nah 3:14 ESV
Whatever your hand finds to do, do it with all your might. —Eccl 9:10
There Is a Time to Work and Not to Work:
The seventh day is the Sabbath; on that day you are to do no work… —Exo 20:8–11 ISV
On Being Idle or Lazy:
If you don't work, you don't eat. —2 Th 3:10 CEV
A roof sags because of laziness. A house leaks because of idle hands. —Eccl 10:18 GW
Benefits:
There is nothing better than to eat, drink, and rejoice. —Eccl 8:15 LEB
Let endurance have its effect, so that you may be complete, lacking nothing. —James 1:4 ISV

Outreach

Outreach can be difficult with family and friends who cast aside Christian values. For such, we have the guidelines to practice agape and tough love. Since we often do not know details, we need to pray for the wisdom of God to know when and how to apply agape and tough love, and when it is time to move on.

> *Avoid those who have knowingly rejected the way. Keep away from every brother*
> *who is idle and does not live according to the teaching you received from us.*
> *Do not associate with them.* — 2 Th 3:6,14; 2 John 1:10; 2 Tim 3:5
> *Encourage each other toward love and good works.* —Heb 10:24 ERV
> *Offer hospitality and entertain strangers—without grumbling.* —1 Pet 4:9 ESV; Heb 13:2

Family

A couple united in marriage will normally reproduce, forming a union called *family*. In the BBI, the roles of husband and wife are defined relative to each other and their family.

Husbands and Wives

> *Do not be yoked together with unbelievers.*
> *For what do righteousness and lawlessness have in common?* —2 Cor 6:14
> *They are no longer two, but one flesh.*
> *What God has joined together, let not man separate.* —Mat 19:6 Darby
> *Marriage is honorable, and the marriage bed undefiled.* —Heb 13:4
> *Husbands, love your wives, even as Christ loved the church.* —Eph 5:25
> *Be considerate of your wives, and treat them with respect.* —1 Pet 3:7 GNB
> *Wives, submit to your husband as to the Lord.* —Eph 5:22–25; 1 Pet 3: 1

A family consists of a father, mother, and children. In a broader sense, family includes brothers and sisters in Christ. Family involves a sacred responsibility from the members.

> *Live in harmony, be sympathetic, love as brothers, be compassionate and humble.*
> *Do not repay evil for evil or insult for insult, but with blessing.* —1 Pet 3:8, 9 ISV
>
> *If anyone does not provide for his relatives, and especially for his immediate family,*
> *he has denied the faith and is worse than an unbeliever.* —1 Tim 5:8 ISV
> *Children, obey your parents.*
> *Honor your father and mother so that it may go well with you.* —Eph 6: 1–3
> *Fathers, do not provoke your children to anger;*
> *instead, bring them up in the discipline and instruction of the Lord.* —Eph 6:4 ESV
> Mothers: *She opens her mouth with wisdom; in her tongue is the law of kindness.*
> *She looks to the ways of her household and does not eat the bread of idleness.* —Prov 31

Proverbs 31 describes an ideal mother and wife. The same passage could be paraphrased to include the father and husband. Read the entire passage for inspiration to allow your God-given talents room to grow and mature for the benefit of your family.

Proverbs 31 shows the freedom of the mother in the home. It should not be interpreted as a one-way street where the mother is a servant to the family. Per biblical instruction, the husband and wife should serve each other.

Inspire and Be Blessed

Blessed are the meek, and they that mourn, for they shall be filled.

The old, discarded shoe has had its day. Now, though meek, humbled, mournful, and deserted, it still has purpose and inspires. That is the objective: an outgoing, inspirational life regardless of the circumstances. From another perspective, no matter your status, give glory to God that you have purpose through His many gifts.

The biblical blessings are a family of challenges with promise. Regardless of our spiritual maturity, there is room for improvement: to make our lives more abundant and full of joy. According to His proven ways, biblical blessings are not a heritage of rights, but accrue to us only if we do these things. To gain understanding for application and benefit, study these verses with reference to a biblical commentary. God's blessings are the ultimate inspiration.

Behaviors with Promise

He began to teach them saying, —Mat 5:2–11

Blessed are:

The POOR in SPIRIT,	*for*	*Theirs is the kingdom of heaven.*
Those who MOURN,	*for*	*They shall be comforted.*
The MEEK (the humble),	*for*	*They will inherit the earth.*
Those who thirst	*for*	*RIGHTEOUSNESS, for They shall be filled.*
The MERCIFUL,	*for*	*They shall be shown mercy.*
The PURE in HEART,	*for*	*They shall see God.*
The PEACEMAKERS,	*for*	*They shall be called sons of God*
The PERSECUTED,	*for*	*Theirs is the kingdom of heaven.*

For Magnified Blessings,
Cherish, Know, and Faithfully Practice
Each of the Golden Virtues of the Fruit of the Spirit

Appendix II
Peace and Joy

Joy is an outward emotion that flows from inward peace. The seeds of peace and joy come to life when we are nurtured by our Maker and we live in harmony with His ways.

Those endearing words, *peace* and *joy*, are mentioned more than five hundred times in the Bible, and they are identified as unique flavors of the fruit of the Spirit. In reviewing the following verses, note how skillfully and thoroughly the Bible provides understanding and a basis for peace and joy.

How magnificent are Your ways, oh Lord!

Basics

If we have food and clothing, we will be content —1 Tim 6:8

You will keep him in perfect peace whose mind is stead on You. —Isa 26:3

When love and faithfulness meet, righteousness and peace kiss each other. —Psa 85:10 ESV

Blessings

Blessed are the peacemakers, for they shall be called sons of God. —Mat 5:9

You shall go with joy and be led out by peace.
The mountains and hills shall break out into song before you,
and all the trees of the field shall clap their hands. —Isa 55:12

Greetings

May the God of peace be with you all. Amen. —Rom 15:33

Brothers rejoice. Aim for restoration, comfort one another, live in peace,
and the God of love and peace will be with you. —2 Cor 13:11 ESV

Be a Happy, Joyful Mate

Always be joyful. Continually be prayerful. In everything be thankful. —1 Th 5:16–18 ISV

Clap your hands. Shout to God with a loud cry of joy. —Psa 47:1 ISV

Take up your tambourines and dance joyfully. —Jer 31:4 GNB

No one will take away your joy. Your joy will be complete. —John 16:22–24

In Everything, Rejoice

You turned my wailing into dancing and clothed me with joy. —Psa 30:11 LEB

Speak to one another with psalms, hymns, and spiritual songs.
Sing and make music in your heart to the Lord, —Eph 5:19 ERV

Rejoice in the Lord always. I will say it again: Rejoice! —Phil 4:4

Now be Content

I learned this secret, so that anywhere, at any time, I am content,
Whether I am full or hungry, whether I have too much or too little. —Phil 4:12 GNB

The Priestly Prayer of Peace

The LORD bless you, and keep you:
The Lord *make his face to shine upon you,*
and be gracious unto you:
The Lord *lift up his countenance upon you,*
and give you peace.
Num 6: 24–26 KJV

(I recited this prayer at our high school graduation. When it was time to recite the prayer, I told the instructor that my mind was blank. Without saying a word, she pushed me onto the stage. I said the prayer without a fault.)

The Marital Sauna Dance

For an exhilarating and stimulating *experience*, play praise music while reviewing the above verses of peace and joy. Let the music and the soothing voice of the peace verses relax your spirit to flow with the gentle Breeze of the Spirit. Then, when fully engulfed in oneness with God's Spirit, plunge into the joy verses of the Bible. The gentle Breeze of the Spirit, so soothing and quieting, now crescendos to whirlwind velocity, carrying your soul to ever-higher levels of delight and bliss.

Ah! This is just the start. A gourmet meal is best enjoyed when shared. Similarly, for maximum effect, do the *Sauna Dance* with your mate. Then, united as one spirit under one God, relax, absorb, and enjoy, for these are God's delightful gifts to you. United as one in peace and joy, your marriage is as good and secure as possible. To expand the delight of the Sauna Dance, share these delightful gifts with all God's children.

To magnify the joy in the sauna experience, reference a concordance for words like *joy, happiness,* and *peace.* Then reference the related verses for context and for their nutritional value. Then let those verses flow over you like refreshing waters on a hot day.

Appendix III
Supporting Math

Insurance Measure 2: Excellence

The equation to determine the number of dollars (or talents) available (A) after investing a fixed principle (P) for a period of (N) years at (i) interest rate is $A = P \times (1 + i)^N$

For example, If you invest \$100 (P = 100) at a 5% growth rate (i = 5% or 0.05), after 3 years, N = 3, your total $A = P \times (1 + i)^N = 100 \times (1 + 0.05)^3 = 100 \times 1.05 \times 1.05 \times 1.05 = \$115.8$.

Insurance Measure 5: Planning
Budgeting

The following is a review of the math that shows the fantastic growth potential of budgeting and saving. We will start with the *Rule of 0.72,* an approximation that relates interest (i) to the doubling period (D). In equation form $i \approx 0.72/D$; similarly, $D \approx 0.72/i$ (the symbol $\approx$ means *about*). For example, an investment earning on average 10% per year (i = 0.1) will double (D) in a little more than seven years (0.72 / 0.1 = 7.2 yrs). A 10% annual interest rate will double almost six times in forty-two years (42 yrs/7.2 yrs/D = 5.8 D). The doubling sequence goes 1 + 1 = 2; 2 + 2 = 4, then 8, 16, 32, 64, and so on. Thus, one dollar will double to 2, then to 4, 8, 16, 32, and 64 dollars in six doubling periods.

There is an interesting anomaly: the savings of one year (\$5,000) invested at 10 percent over forty-two years provides \$64,000 more than saving \$5,000 per year (\$210,000 total) in a coffee can for forty-two years. That reality illustrates the power of compounded returns resulting from a series of doubling periods.

The math: from above, $A = P \times (1 + i)^N = 5,000 (1.1)^{42} = 5,000 (54.8) = \$273,818$
$$\$5,000 \times 42 \text{ yrs} = \$210,000. \quad \$274,000 - \$210,000 = \$64.000$$

As illustrated above, the compounded value of time explodes when savings are yearly. You don't have to understand the math, but you need to realize that the results are certain if the math is correctly applied.

The Sum (S) of an Amount (A) invested at Interest (i) every year for (n) years is— $S = A [(1 + i)^n – 1]/i$

Examples

1. Assume that you invest \$5,000 annually for 42 years at a 10% growth rate (the market average). How much will you have at the end of 42 years?

    Your investment with compounded interest will be worth about 2.7 million dollars.

    $S = A [(1 + i)^n – 1]/i. = \$5,000 [(1 + 0.1)^{42} - 1]/0.1 = (\$5,000 \times 53.76)/0.1 = \$2,688,185$

2. Assume the same calculation, only at an aggressive 15% annual growth rate.

    At 15%, the net (S) of savings and interest after 42 years is—

    $S = \$5,000[(1 + 0.15)^{42} – 1]/0.15 = 5,000 (354.2 – 1)/0.15] \approx \$11,773,000$

3. At a nominal 5% growth rate, you will have about $\$5,000[(1 + 0.05)^{42} – 1]/0.05 = \$676,000$

    At the end of 42 years, you will have invested \$5,000 x 42 or \$210,000.

    Note the dramatic difference that results from only 10 percentage points of extra effort.

LORD
Make me an instrument of your peace,
Where there is hatred, let me sow love,
Where there is injury, pardon,
Where there is doubt, faith,
Where there is darkness, light,
And where there is sadness, joy.

Divine Master
Grant that I may not so much seek
To be consoled as to console,
To be understood as to understand,
To be loved as to love.
For it is in giving that we receive,
It is in pardoning that we are pardoned,
And it is in dying that we are
Born to eternal life.

✝

Prayer of St Francis of Assisi

Printed in the United States
by Baker & Taylor Publisher Services